Close Encounters
in the Royal Mile

To my wife Helen and my daughter Sheenagh, who were most tolerant and understanding while I was carrying out the research into this work; and to my grandchildren, Sarah, Emma and Andrew, all of whom I hope may find this book of interest when they are old enough to understand it; and to my friends Bob, John and Ian who (unknown to them) were responsible for initiating the idea.

All profits from this publication will be donated to the Scottish Down's Syndrome Association, Edinburgh, in dedication to my daughter, Sheenagh, who was born with the Down's Syndrome condition.

The Author: Alastair M.R. Hardie is a retired welfare officer of British Telecom, and his main interest is now the history of his native city. He is particularly drawn to the content of this book since many of his ancestors variously lived in Chessel's Court, Carrubber's Close, and White Horse Close.

Along with his wife Helen he has written another book, entitled *Why Me?*, the life story of their daughter, Sheenagh, as seen through her eyes (published by Excalibur Press, London).

Close Encounters in the Royal Mile

*A walking guide, with
an historical background
to all the closes, wynds,
pends and lands, including
a history of the Nor' Loch*

Alastair M. R. Hardie

JOHN DONALD PUBLISHERS LTD
EDINBURGH

Cover photographs

Top: View from Advocate's Close in the High Street
Middle: Site of the old Nor' Loch
Bottom: Paisley Close in the High Street
Background: From Castlehill to Lawnmarket

All photographs are by the author.

ISBN 0 85976 414 1

Phototypeset by Westkey Ltd, Falmouth, Cornwall
Printed in Great Britain by Bell & Bain Ltd., Glasgow

Other John Donald books about Edinburgh and District

Thomas Begbie's Edinburgh
D. Patterson & J. Rock

Edinburgh through the Lens
Ian Torrance

Edinburgh: The New Town
Ian Nimmo

Morningside
Charles J. Smith

A French King at Holyrood
Lord Mackenzie-Stuart

Canonmills and Inverleith
Joyce M. Wallace

Historic Houses of Edinburgh
Joyce M. Wallace

**Further Traditions
of Trinity and Leith**
Joyce M. Wallace

The Port of Leith
Sue Mowat

The Life and Times of Leith
James Marshall

Discovering The Water of Leith
Hamish Coghill

Newhaven on Forth
Tom McGowran

Discovering the Pentland Hills
Jim Crumley

Contents

page

Diagrams   **vi-vii**

Prologue   **viii**

Part 1   **Introduction**   **1**

The historical background of the Old Town's Royal Mile and the origin of its closes etc.

Part 2   **The Royal Mile Closes etc.**   **11**

Details of the history of each of the current closes, in the form of a walking tour down the North side of the Royal Mile from Castlehill to the Canongate returning via the south side.

Part 3   **Other Points of Interest in the Royal Mile**   **77**

A brief history of many of the old buildings the visitor will pass in addition to the tour illustrated under Part 2.

Part 4   **The Nor' Loch**   **91**

The history of the defence loch which existed several centuries before Princes Street Gardens had been constructed and down to which most of the old closes descended

Part 5   **Appendix A**   **99**

A list of 497 names of closes, wynds, entries, or courts either no longer in existence or renamed many, many times. The current name is shown against those which are known. Included is a list of 30 unidentified closes.

Part 6   **Appendix B**   **113**

A list of most of the current close, court, etc. names quoting the previous name/names alongside.

Part 7   **Appendix C**   **117**

A list of 35 closes' etc. names in existence when William Edgar's first complete and accurate plan of Edinburgh was published in 1742, and still retaining the same names today, and 62 others long since obsolete but appearing on the plan.

Bibliography   **119**

Epilogue   **120**

Index   **121**

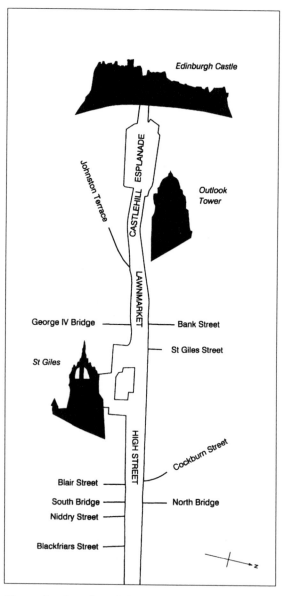

Diagram for orientation only: from the Castle to Blackfriars Street.

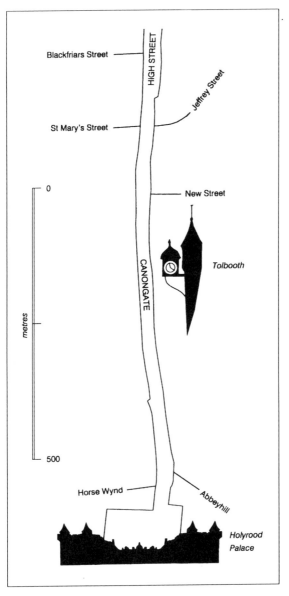

Diagram for orientation only: from Blackfriars Street to Holyrood.

Prologue

My research into the old historic closes, wynds, pends, courts, etc., of Edinburgh's Royal Mile extends back over two to three years. I first became interested one evening when friends and I parked the car at the foot of the Canongate and proceeded to ascend the Royal Mile, stopping to read the brief bronze information plaques erected in the entries to most, but not all, of the closes. This extended walk through the mists of time was sufficient to whet my appetite into finding out more about the historical background of each close. And this I endeavoured to do by reading many old (and new) books, papers and records on the subject. I found that, to my knowledge, no book had been published specifically to give the visitor (or even an interested Edinburgh resident!) as much insight as possible into the Royal Mile closes, and no comprehensive (or near comprehensive) list of all the names ever given to the closes, courts, etc., down through the centuries had ever been compiled. This I attempted to do and was amazed when the complete list totalled 497 obsolete names and 30 unidentified names (as quoted in Part 5 – Appendix A) and 83 current names – a surprising overall total of 610.

It will no doubt be appreciated that the authenticity of this publication must not be taken as irrefutable although every care has been taken to make it as accurate as possible.

For convenience I have divided the booklet into reference Parts as shown in the list of contents.

While carrying out this research it was of particular interest to me to learn that my grandfather was born in Chessels Court in 1864 and that he and other ancestors had lived in Carrubber's and White Horse Closes towards the latter part of the 19th Century. Also towards the conclusion of my research a cousin sent me a small photo-copy of William Edgar's map of the Old Town, dated 1742. On visiting the Edinburgh Room of the Edinburgh Central Library I obtained a larger photocopy which contained the names of all the closes etc., in existence at that date (as quoted in Part 7, Appendix C) but unsuitable for reproduction. This to me was 'the pot of gold at the end of the rainbow!'

In addition I thought that the reader might be interested in the various definitions of the words closes, courts, etc. On consulting the Scots Dictionary for a description of these places we find:

Close: *An enclosure, or courtyard, an entry, a vennel, passageway, alley or entry back or front to a tenement, a passageway, giving access to the common stair'.* (Originally in Edinburgh's Old Town a close was a dividing lane between gardens but later as land became scarce in the 17th century they were filled in and built upon and the narrow lanes leading down to them from the Royal Mile were then called 'closes').

Wynd: *A narrow winding street, open from both ends.*

Court: *A courtyard surrounded by buildings.*

Pend: *An arched passageway or entry especially one leading into the back-court of a block of houses.*

Entry: *An alley or covered passage usually in or between houses.*

Land: *A holding of land; a building site; a building on this; a tenement or block of flats.*

Although we in Scotland are familiar with the word 'close' as being a narrow short cut to the rear of a row of dwellings or their yards visitors from across the Border might be at home with the following more familiar variety of names depending on which part of the country they come from:

Alley (found in many places); *Gullet* (Staffs); *Gulley* (Monmouthshire); *Jigger* (Liverpool); *Jitty* (Notts); *Loke* (Norfolk); *Lanes* (Brighton); *Opes* (Portland and Dorset); *Rows* (Great Yarmouth and Norfolk); *Score* (Lowestoft area); *Snicket* (Yorkshire, Liverpool and Herefordshire); *Twitchett* (Notts); *Twitten* (Sussex); *Ginnel* (Yorkshire) and *Cambrill* (origin unknown) and the following further selection all of which are used in the Sussex area — *Cross, The Diplocks, Folly, Nest, Reach, Strip, View, Way and Walk...*

How fortunate we in Scotland are to have but one simple word... *Close!*

In conclusion I extend my grateful thanks to Miss Joyce Wallace, author of books about districts of Edinburgh, for her careful and accurate checking of my manuscripts and for her very helpful suggestions.

Alastair Hardie
Edinburgh

PART ONE
Introduction

Once visitors from many foreign parts have finished clambering all over the ramparts of Edinburgh Castle (Scotland's top tourist attraction) a large percentage of them wend their way down the Old Town's Royal Mile to inspect the curious variety of shops and places of historical interest. Here much of Scotland's tumultuous history was acted out. And here also is the fascinating setting for five City museums—The Writers' Museum; The Museum of Childhood; The Brass Rubbing Centre; Huntly House Museum and The People's Story. But then, the Royal Mile is a museum in itself . . .

The 'Old Town' was known as the 'Royal Mile' since at the top inside the Castle was a palace and the mile led down to the Palace of Holyroodhouse at the foot. The distance from the inside of the Castle drawbridge to the entrance door of Holyrood Palace measures 1 mile 106 yards.

The Old Town originally developed as two separate burghs—that of Edinburgh spreading downhill from the Castle, and Canongate climbing uphill from the Abbey of Holyrood. By the early 17th century, the linked roadway of the Royal Mile had become the main route, with markets on wider sections. Before the New Town was built, pressure on space in the Old Town resulted in a dense concentration of tall buildings to the north and south of the Royal Mile, separated only by narrow closes.

Improvements in the 18th and 19th centuries maintained the Old Town's role as the core of the City and as a definable community in its own right. It has inherited a rich environment full of historic buildings. Now, with many derelict buildings and neglected areas, the next decade is being seen as a vital period in which to get the area into good shape to meet its next century.

The Royal Mile owes its name to the long succession of

Royal personages whose footsteps trod the area in the past, namely Scottish kings, Queens, Princes and Princesses from the days of David I to James VI and I.

It was originally constructed naturally by a ridge of lava which flowed eastwards 350 million years ago from the (now extinct) volcano or rock on which the Castle was built. As a result of recent excavations it has been discovered that the rock was the site of an encampment as long ago as the Iron Age (500 years BC) and also during the Roman invasion.

The mile itself is divided into five sections:

Castlehill

Lawnmarket (once 'Landmarket' where produce was sold—milk, meat, vegetables, linen and wool cloth);

High Street (known at one time as 'Plainstones' because of the flagged or paved part of the street);

Canongate (in Scotland 'gate' applied to a way or a road; the Canons were members of the St Augustine's order of Holyrood Abbey; it was along the Canongate that the Canons walked to the City), and

Abbey Strand.

Edinburgh was at one time a walled city surrounded by a 30-foot-high, 6-foot-thick defence wall containing 7 fortified gateways which were opened at dawn and closed at dusk. The Flodden Wall was built after the defeat of the Scottish Army in 1513. A later wall was the Telfer Wall; sections of both can be seen at the Heriot Place Vennel.

Early in the 15th Century the first tenements were erected inside the City walls. They were crowded close together round the Castle for protection and because of the terrain which restricted building on the Eastern slope. For safety's sake no-one dared build outside the perimeter. Streets were narrow, gardens and closes filled up and there was no alternative but to build upwards in cramped conditions. Dunghills piled up and as swine were kept by many householders in pens under outside stairs, plague was rife. To the North the defences consisted of a man-made Loch called the Nor' Loch covering the site of Princes Street Gardens and formed by a dam where the North Bridge now stands.

There was literally no drainage or plumbing and street cleaning was overlooked. At about 10p.m. every night the familiar sounds of 'gardy-loo' (from the French 'gardez l'eau' or 'beware water') could be heard the length of the street, to warn folks in the street below that a deluge of 'slops' was about to fall from the heights. 'Haud yer hand' shouted back pedestrians as they scrambled for cover. Pigs rummaged about among the debris in the gutter; passers-by picked their way carefully through it and the stench permeated into the houses. Many houses burned paper to fumigate the rooms because of this. In the early morning at 7a.m. scavengers moved slowly through the street to clean up the previous evening's discard. However the rubbish from Saturdays merged with that of Sundays and was not cleaned up until Monday morning! The popular fiddle tune—'The Floors o' Edinburgh'—recalls, not as we might expect the delights of the Royal Botanic Garden blooms, but in fact the nickname for the stench which emanated from the open sewers between the tenements in those days of 'gardy-loo'!

Over the centuries people lived in fine high houses, at one time the tallest in Europe (Europe's first skyscrapers, some as high as 16 storeys, including basements, because of the steep slopes) in 'lands' which rose over the waters of the Nor' Loch to the North and down to the Grassmarket and Cowgate to the South.

The population was of a mixed crowd—lawyers, merchants, aristocrats, physicians, booksellers, wrights, farmers, tavern owners, tradesmen and ordinary folk. Some of their occupations sound strange to our modern job

3

descriptions—money scrivener, inspector of window lights, mantua or mantie maker (ie, dressmaker), clothes cleaner, gumflower maker, setter of elegant rooms, fringe manufacturer, extractor, and harpsickord and spinet maker.

One chilling Edinburgh legend was that of MAJOR THOMAS WEIR, Commander of the Town Guard and a strict Presbyterian lay preacher who lived with his sister Grizel in an old house in the West Bow then at the junction of the Lawnmarket with the present Johnston Terrace.

After a severe illness, in 1669 Major Weir confessed in partnership with his sister to acts of incest, bestiality, sorcery and wizardry. There followed a series of rumours that he had entered into a pact with the Devil and that the twisted stick he carried with him was his sinister servant. Both he and Grizel were imprisoned, tried and sentenced to death. His sister was hanged in the Grassmarket in 1670 and he was burned alive. For over a century afterwards his ghost was said to gallop down the High Street on a headless black horse surrounded by flames. Grizel was also spotted in the Old Town with her flesh blackened and her face in a weird grimace. Their house was demolished in 1878.

As recently as the late 19th and early 20th century street traders common in the High Street had peculiar but perhaps descriptive names. Among them was Tam Simpson, a real character known as 'Coconut Tam'. He was a kenspeckle humpy wee man with a frayed bowler hat several sizes too large, adorned with a sprig of heather, and a jacket so large that his hands were concealed in the sleeves. His shirt collar was of the fly-away type. He eaked out a meagre living selling coconuts and vegetables—his battle cry being 'Coco-nit, Coco-nit; Come an' buy, ha'penny a bit.' He spread his wares out in front of him—hairy coconuts, potatoes and sometimes onions.

Several other characters seen in the city streets at the

same time were Pie Davie, Moodie Heels, Mutton Hole Willie, Betsy Mustard, Gramophone Granny, and a Newhaven fishwife—'The Buckie Wife'—who sat in the Lawnmarket in traditional dress beside a heavy wicker basket selling 'portions of boiled whulks & buckies'. It was not an uncommon sight to see a crowd standing round her on a Saturday afternoon well into the 1950s, picking winkles with a pin!

Between 1560 and 1760 those living in this area trebled from 10,000 to 30,000; by the mid 1800s this figure had risen to about 50,000.

The last quarter of the 17th Century saw an important period of rebuilding—many of the older tenements were rebuilt, and timber-fronted and thatched houses, with wooden balconies and stairs projecting into the closes and the High Street, thus blocking out the light, were mostly removed.

Eventually this inner city burst at the seams, and in 1767 work on the North Bridge was begun to link the Old Town with the New Town to the North. The well-to-do moved out of the Old to live in the New leaving the Old to deteriorate to a large slum.

In the 1930s steps were taken to stop the rot by those fearful that Edinburgh would lose its heritage, and therefore a large regeneration and rebuilding programme was introduced to restore the city to its former grandeur.

The Old Town is still the heart of Edinburgh, housing about 6,500 people. There, tourists from all over the world mingle with the citizens of Edinburgh and can catch up with the history of the old buildings. Some of the narrow closes and old houses are still there. Plaques on the walls tell the inquisitive who lived there, what happened, and at almost every turn-off the High Street a glimpse of other buildings framed in a close mouth can be caught with a sense of their steepness as they plunge into the Grassmarket, into the Cowgate, and towards Princes Street.

Many of the old closes had no history of note apart from the ancestry of those who dwelt in them. Others had stories to tell, some sinister, some gruesome, some historic, but all of interest.

Those on the north side of the Royal Mile led down to the old Nor' Loch, at one time an impassable fetid marsh and receptacle of many sewers, rubbish, dead cats and dogs, and possibly the escape routes of many blackguards. The smuggling of contraband from overseas landed at Figgate Burn and passed through Lady Stair's, Baxter's or Advocates' Closes to cellars and other resting places.

The names of the closes, wynds, pends, and courts have, in almost every case, been derived from that of the chief resident, or from those who built or owned the tenement or nearby land. Some of these have remained unchanged throughout the centuries, such as Lochend Close, Jackson's Close or Bell's Wynd. Others have changed completely down the ages as the owners came and went as shown in Part 5, Appendix A.

In some cases a special interest or peculiarity gave rise to the name, such as 'The Stripping Close', 'Plainstane Close' or 'Stinking Close' (which demands no explanation!)—all of which are long since gone—or 'White Horse Close'.

Originally closes were known by spoken name only, as names were not printed on them. Therefore the original lists were prepared phonetically and not to true spelling. In 1790 however, the Town Council made a rule that the names of the old closes should be painted over the entrances. During the mid-19th century others were swept away as new buildings or wider and airier streets, such as Cockburn Street, came along. Their locations can now only be traced on William Edgar's old city map of 1742 as mentioned in the

Prologue. The construction of George IV Bridge and the Mound caused the disappearance of several of these; one, Libberton's Wynd, could at that time be traced back to 1474.

There are today in existence over the length of the Royal Mile, 11 courts, 3 wynds, 1 pend, 3 entries, 4 lands and 61 closes.

It is interesting and pleasing to note that before the end of the 20th century the Royal Mile is to be given a new look and will thus be reinstated as one of the most attractive streets in Europe. The proposals will mean that the volume and pace of traffic using the historic thoroughfare will be reduced, thereby improving its environment and its safety for pedestrians. There will also be improvements to the appearance of the street, with tree planting, improvements to lamps, and new street furniture.

In addition to this project the historic closes are to be given a much needed facelift, including lighting improvements, cleaning of graffiti, repaving in natural stone, and building repairs. Many of the closes are very narrow and steep, and people do not like to venture down them, although they form useful pedestrian links in the Old Town. Among the first closes to be given a facelift are World's End Close, Old Fishmarket Close, Advocate's Close, Anchor Close, and Old Tolbooth Wynd.

As already indicated, it is well known that the Mile is a link with Edinburgh's historic past, and a key component of any visit to the city. The aim is to make it an attractive safe area, especially for tourists, who provide vital business to local traders, and an asset to be enjoyed by all of Edinburgh, whether as a place to live, a business house, or to visit.

The project is due to be funded by Lothian Regional Council, Lothian and Edinburgh Enterprise Ltd, and the Edinburgh Old Town Renewal Trust.

No guide of this kind, however, would be deemed

complete without mention of 'the father of town planning'—SIR PATRICK GEDDES.

Born at Ballater in 1854, poor health prevented his attendance at school before the age of 8. He therefore received much of his early education from his father. After leaving school he worked in a bank for 18 months but also practised drawing and cabinet-making. He tried botany at Edinburgh University in 1874 for one week(!) then moved to London to study under Huxley. Research took him to Brittany, Paris, and Mexico. For ten years he was Demonstrator of Botany at Edinburgh University. He and his wife lived in a slum in the Grassmarket and later in James' Court. He established student hostels which were run by the students themselves. In 1888 he became Professor of Botany at University College, Dundee, but Edinburgh remained his base. He built Ramsay Garden in 1893 on the site of the poet, Allan Ramsay's house. Locals called it 'goose-pie' but it is a shrine for town-planners from all parts of the world, being the earliest example that we know of organised town planning. He started gardens in the Grassmarket and on Johnston Terrace to bring nature into the lives of ordinary people. He owned the Outlook Tower or Camera Obscura (built in the 17th century) from 1892, and he created one of the first museums that gave people an insight into other parts of the world; it contained rooms on geography, history and natural science. He was renowned as the great modern pioneering master of townscape who contributed so much to the conservation of old Edinburgh in the closing years of the 19th and early 20th century. He did a great deal towards the rehabilitation of the Royal Mile by remodelling buildings in order to entice students and University lecturers back to the Old Town.

Under his influence the 4th Marquis of Bute preserved and restored Acheson House (built 1633) in 1937 to the plans of the architect Robert Hurd (1905–1963). Geddes recognised how much of the medieval Old Town was lost, how much had by chance survived, and how much was at risk. By the foresight and vision of Geddes, and later, of Robert Hurd, the rot was stopped. This was most apparent in the restoration of the 17th- and 18th-century humble Canongate tenements.

He toured the world extensively, lecturing, with exhibitions and city plans, and in 1919 became Professor of Civics and Sociology in the University of Bombay. Ill health compelled him to leave in 1924, and he settled in the South of France, where he died in 1932.

His interest in restoring the Old Town is marked by a *Heritage Trail* which extends over a mile-long route taking in:

> Ramsay Garden, Outlook Tower, Castlehill School (now the Scotch Whisky Heritage Centre), Riddle's Court, Mylne's Court, James' Court, Burn's Land, Blackie House, Old Assembly Close, Chessel's Court, Moray House, Huntly House, Dunbar's Close garden, and other places outside the Royal Mile.

Visitors are invited to spot the 'Heritage Trail' plaques posted along the route.

Sir Patrick Geddes was indeed Edinburgh's greatest all-round citizen.

PART TWO
The Royal Mile Closes, etc.

For those interested in the history of such places this guide, or tour, has been devised to commence at the North side of Castlehill and to progress Eastwards via the north sides of the Lawnmarket and High Street to the Canongate. The number quoted after each close name relates, where information has been available, to the appropriate street number.

The last part of the Royal Mile—Abbey Strand—has not been touched upon, since it contains no closes, wynds, courts, etc.

By crossing to the south side of the Canongate the visitor can then ascend the Royal Mile and proceed back to Castlehill.

En route all the closes, etc., will be described in sequence in as much detail as it has been possible to gather from old records; as mentioned earlier some have no history of note apart from the ancestry of those who dwelt in them, while others have tales to tell. Of these perhaps the most interesting are Mary King's Close, Allan's Close, Bell's Wynd, Brodie's Close, Brown's Close (Golfer's Land), and Riddle's Court/Close—but let the visitor be the judge of these.

In order to add variety to the tour, there is included at Part 3 a chapter on the brief history of other places of interest which the visitor will pass on the way.

Also in sequence these are:

Descending Eastward on the North side of the Royal Mile	*Ascending Westward on the South side of the Royal Mile*
Outlook Tower	Queensberry House
Gladstone's Land	Acheson House
City Chambers	Huntly House
Moubray House	Moray House
John Knox House	Museum of Childhood
Netherbow Port	Tron Kirk

Canongate Tolbooth
Canongate Church

Mercat Cross
St Giles' Cathedral
Parliament House & Square
(originally Close)
Edinburgh Tolbooth
Highland Church of
Tolbooth St John's
Cannonball House

Closes, etc., On the North Side of the Royal Mile

Castlehill
(Ramsay Lane)
Semple's Close—541
Skinner's Close
Jollie's Close

Lawnmarket
Mylne's Court—517
James Court (West,
Mid, East)—491
(Gladstone Land)
Lady Stair's
Close—477
Wardrop's
Court—437.
(George IV
Bridge/Bank St)

High Street
(St. Giles St)
Byres' Close—373
Advocate's
Close—357
Writer's Court
(Leading to

Warriston
Close)—315
(City
Chambers)—Mary
King's Close
Site of entry to
Allan's Close
(Closed 1932)—269
Site of entry to
Craig's Close
(Closed 1932)—265
Site of entry to Old
Post Office Close
(Closed 1932)
(City Collector's
Office)
Anchor Close—241
Geddes Entry—233
North Foulis
Close—229
Old Stamp Office
Close—221
Lyon's Close—215
Jackson's Close—209

Fleshmarket
  Close—199
(Cockburn St)
(North/South
  Bridge)
Carrubber's
  Close—135
Bishop's Close—129
North Gray's
  Close—125
Morrison's
  Close—117
Bailie Fyfe's
  Close—107
Paisley Close—101
Chalmer's Close—81
Monteith's
  Close—61
Trunk's Close—55
Hope's Court
(John Knox House)
(Netherbow)
Baron Maule's
  Close—13

Canongate

(Jeffrey St)
(Cranston St)
Morocco land—273
Mid Common

Close—269
(New St)
Bible Land—185
Gladstone
  Court—181
Old Tolbooth
  Wynd—165
Dunbar's
  Close—137
Panmure Close—129
Little Lochend
  Close—115
Lochend Close—105
Reid's Court
  (Canongate
  Manse)—95
Campbell's
  Close—87
Brown's Close
  (Golfer's
  Land)—81/79
Forsyth's Close
  (Gloucester
  Gate)—57
Galloway Entry
  (Whiteford
  House)—53
WhiteHorse
  Close—31

Closes etc., In the South Side of the Royal Mile

Canongate

Vallence's Entry—72
Reid's Close—80
Bull's Close—100
(ajacent to Huntly
House museum is
the original
doorway taken
from ANCHOR
Close in 1932 and
rebuilt here in 1937)
Bakehouse
Close—146
Sugarhouse
Close—160
St. John's Pend—188
Old Playhouse
Close—196
Chessel's Court
—240
Gibb's Close—250
Gullan's Close—264
(St Mary's St)

High Street

World's End
Close—10
Tweeddale
Court—14
Fountain Close—22
Hyndford's
Close—34
South Gray's
Close—40
(Museum of
Childhood)
Toddrick's Wynd
(Blackfriar's St)
Melrose Close—66
(within the Scandic
Hotel)
Cant's Close—70
(within the Scandic
Hotel).
Dickson's Close—80
(within the Scandic
Hotel)
(Niddry St)
(Tron Church)
(Hunter Square)
Stevenlaw's
Close—132
New Assembly
Close—142
Bell's Wynd—146
Burnet's Close—156
Covenant
Close—162
Old Assembly
Close—172
Borthwick's
Close—186
Old Fishmarket
Close—190
(St. Giles' Cathedral)
(George IV Bridge)

Lawnmarket

Brodie's Close—304
Fisher's Close—312

Riddle's
  Court/Close—322

Blair's Close
(Castle)

Castlehill
Boswell's
  Court—352

Summary

	South Side	North Side	Total
Closes	24	37	61
Wynds	2	1	3
Courts	4	7	11
Entries	1	2	3
Pends	1	–	1
Lands	–	4	4
	32	51	83
'Houses'	6	3	9

Closes, etc., In the North Side of the Royal Mile

Castlehill

Outlook Tower—see Page 77

Semple's Close (541)

This close is now empty and barred up, having a derelict tenement at the rear. It dates back to 1638. It was occupied prior to 1734 by Lady Semple, widow of Francis, the 8th Lord Semple (or Sempill). This family was interesting in that one of the ladies gave shelter in the house to some Catholics when they were being hunted. The family maintained a loyalty to Mary, Queen of Scots, and one of the 'four Mary's' became the wife of a Lord Sempill. The property passed out of the Semple tenure in 1760 but still retains the family name. It was at one time called Williamson's Close, after an Advocate of that name, in 1860.

Skinner's Close

The close was named after the Skinner's land houses built by the Incorporation of Skinners and Furriers of Edinburgh. Wm. Brown, skinner and Boxmaster (i.e. Treasurer) of the company had his house here.

Jollie's Close

A tenement here was owned by Patrick Jollie and later Alexander Jollie, writer, in 1859. The close is of no historical interest.

Lawnmarket

Mylne's Court (517)

Designed and built by Architect Robert Mylne of Balfargie in 1690, this was a first attempt to substitute an open square for the narrow closes. The northerly land dates from 1590 and looms high over the Mound. Mylne was His Majesty's Master Mason to the Royal House of Stewart in 1668 and did much work for Charles II—he also assisted Sir William Bruce in the design and building of Holyroodhouse. His son built Blackfriars Bridge, London, and was surveyor of St Paul's Cathedral. The houses were at one time occupied by the officers of Bonnie Prince Charlie. The old buildings which formed the west side of the Court were demolished in 1883.

The north and south blocks were restored and the east range rebuilt by the University of Edinburgh between 1966 and 1970. It is now a hall of residence. This work was made possible by generous friends of the University.

James' Court (West, Mid, East) (491)

James Brownhill, wright and speculative builder, built this courtyard in 1725/7 after removing the existing closes and modestly called it by his Christian name but it was also in the past known as Brownhill's Court. David Hume, philosopher and historian, and James Boswell were residents in the western block (since burned down in 1857). Boswell entertained Dr Samuel Johnson as a guest in 1773.

Let us pause for a short while to give mention to the said DAVID HUME described by the Duke of Edinburgh as 'one of Scotland's most brilliant sons'. He was without doubt one of the most influential thinkers of all time.

Born in Edinburgh's High Street in 1711 in a house yards from the former Sheriff Court building (soon to be the High Court Building) he studied at Edinburgh University but did not graduate. He became a lawyer but suffered depression. In 1739 he published his *Treatise of Human Nature* but had to wait until 1741 when his *Essays, Moral and Political* gained him true recognition. He became part of a new school of economics and political thought led by his friend, Adam Smith. He was rejected for the Professorship of Moral Philosophy at Edinburgh University in 1744, possibly because of his new theories. He became Keeper of the Advocates' Library in 1752, the year when his *Political Discourses* secured his fame. He died in 1776.

It is hoped at some time in the not too distant future that a statue of national and international significance in his honour will be erected in the Royal Mile possibly near to the location of the house in which he was born.

Sir Patrick Geddes 19th century "father of town planning" also lived here and had two blocks of flats protruding into the court designed to let light into all windows from east or west and in order to give each family a sheltered balcony and a place to hang and dry washing. The courtyard declined about 1790 with the rise of the New Town and the buildings were destroyed by fire in 1857. They were later rebuilt by David Bryce architect of Fettes College.

The court has three entries from the Lawnmarket—West, Mid and East.

The eastward entry of the original close belonged in 1631 to Sir Thomas Gladstane, ancestor of the statesman, and in 1755 was in the possession of William Gladstane, surgeon. Other residents over the years were the Earl of Aberdeen, Lord Bankton, Sir John Clerk of Penicuik and Ilay Campbell, Lord President of the Court of Session.

Gladstone's Land—see Page 77

Lady Stair's Close & House (477) and the Writers' Museum

The house was built in 1622 by Sir William Gray of Pittendrum, a wealthy merchant, and was originally called Lady Gray's Close after his wife Geida, sister of Sir John Smith, Lord Provost in 1643. Both her own and her husband's initials are carved on the lintel of the entrance—WG & GS—with the words 'Feare the Lord and depart from evil'. Not a lot is known about William Gray, other than that

Lady Stair's Close looking towards Lady Stair's House in the Lawnmarket.

he enjoyed some prominence as a merchant in the City and that he backed the wrong horse in the Wars of the Covenant, an error of judgment possibly responsible for his early demise in 1648. But it was unlike Mr Gray to make errors. In matters regarding his house he was meticulous. In particular he took

Lady Stair's House and Museum (now 'The Writers' Museum').

specific steps to ensure his safety against intruders. It was the stair itself that was his 'burglar alarm'.

You only have to experience going up or down the worn steps of a tenement to appreciate the virtue of stairs that have all their steps of uniform height. Once your first few steps have established the pattern you can virtually run up or down them. However, throw in a couple of 'rogue' steps to break the pattern and you have every chance of breaking an ankle.

This was the principle of the 'trip' stair, an example of which William Gray had built into his house. As an additional precaution his stair spiralled clockwise thus a right-handed defending swordsman would have the advantage over a right-handed ascending sword wielding intruder! The house had a terraced garden which descended to the edge of the Nor' Loch, then a receptacle for all kinds of refuse and impurity, and which housed water rats and eels. The close and house acquired its present name and form when it passed into the possession of Elizabeth, Countess Dowager of Stair in 1719; it was originally a cul-de-sac. Lady Stair was widow of John, 1st Earl of Stair, and daughter of Sir John Dundas of Newliston. She died in 1731. Before Bank Street was laid down in 1798 and on the construction of the earthen Mound from Princes Street to the High Street, a thoroughfare was cut through the garden, making the close the principal communication between the Lawnmarket and Hanover Street, then the Western extremity of the New Town. Robert Burns lived on the East side of the close during his first visit to Edinburgh in 1786.

In 1897 the mansion house was bought and restored by Archibald Philip the 5th Earl of Rosebery in pseudo-medieval style, according to the ideas of Sir Patrick Geddes, and was gifted to the City in 1907. It is now a museum of Scottish literary figures, having a unique collection of relics and manuscripts of Robert Burns, Sir Walter Scott and Robert Louis Stevenson, and it receives many visitors over the years. It has recently been renamed the 'Writers Museum'.

Wardrop's Court (437)

John Wardrop, mason, wright and burgess of the City built a tenement here in 1790. Prior to him it was occupied by the Incorporation of Baxters (i.e. Bakers) of Edinburgh and was known as Middle Baxters' Close. The entrance is guarded overhead by four carved dragon bracket figures and on the

Carved dragon bracket figures 'guarding' the entrance to Wardrop's Court.

inside access is obtainable to Lady Stair's Close. In past years it was popular as the residential quarters of various University professors. The land was restored and modernised in 1950 by Robert Hurd for the Duke of Hamilton. Blackie House is on the North Side of this court.

High Street

Byres' Close (373)

Originally known as Lauder's Close and Malcolme's Close. Dates back to the 16th century and is named after John Byres, a wealthy merchant, bailie, City Treasurer and Old Provost (died 1629). His son, Sir John Byres of Coats, inherited property here from his father. The close at one time housed church and legal dignitaries and merchant princes. The Bishop of Orkney, Adam Bothwell, lived here. He, as Commendator of Holyrood and Lord of Session, married Mary Queen of Scots to Lord Bothwell in 1567 after Lord Darnley's death. He later crowned James VI at Stirling after Queen Mary's abdication. Although his house is in this close it can only be seen from Advocate's Close.

Advocate's Close (357)

Originally known as Cant's Close, Home's Close and
Stewart's Close) This is one of the most photographed views
in Edinburgh's Old Town believed to date from 1544 and
the last to offer an attractive clear view from the High Street
to Princes Street and the Scott Monument. It has the narrow-
ness and steepness typical of the Old Town closes. It was
once so narrow that residents could almost shake hands with
those opposite! In its early days it housed the mansion of Sir
John Scougal, painter of William III and Queen Mary, and
also of Bishop Bothwell who became Abbot of Holyroodhouse in 1570 (see the entry under Byre's Close regarding
sight of his house). But it was named after Sir James Stewart
of Goodtrees who resided here between 1692 and 1713. He
was the last Lord Advocate of Scotland in office at the time
of the Restoration, the Revolution and the Union. A supporter of the House of Orange, he was hated by the Jacobites
who nicknamed him 'Jamie Wylie'. He originally inherited
his house from his father also Sir James Stewart, Provost in
1648 at the time of Cromwell's visit to the City. Another
advocate, Andrew Crosbie, the prototype of Counsellor
Pleydell in Scott's *Guy Mannering*, also lived in the close.

Writers' Court (leading to Warriston Close) (315)

Both were incorporated into the extension of the City Chambers in the 1930s. Near this spot John Knox lived in a manse
from 1560 to 1566. The Writers to HM Signet had their hall
and library in Writers' Court in 1699 and the court also held
the Clerihugh's Tavern where Counsellor Pleydell relaxed
from his work in Parliament House in *High Jinks*. Here also
was the publishing firm of W. & R. Chambers.

Warriston's Close took its name from Wariston's Land,
the house of Sir Archibald Johnstoun (later Lord Warriston),
a judge who lived in the vicinity between 1611–63. He was

a leading Covenanter and principal framer of the National Covenant, first signed in Greyfriar's Church in 1638; he was betrayed and executed in 1663 having been a martyr who suffered at the hands of the Cavalier Government. He took his title from the estate of Warynston near Currie, not to be confused with the Warriston district of Canonmills. His uncle Sir Thomas Craig of Riccarton, Currie, owned the house before him when the close was known as Craig's Close.

City Chambers—see Page 77

Mary King's Close (within the City Chambers)

This is probably the most well-known close in the High Street, yet it does not appear on any street map, simply because it lies beneath the City Chambers! It is possible, by arrangement with City Chambers' staff, to have a guided tour of the close and experience what Edinburgh's High Street was like long ago. Some Edinburgh folks think that an entire street exists beneath the present High Street complete with medieval shops and tenements—sadly that's not the case. The official guide can take you by lift down to this forgotten street preserved in a time capsule. After leaving the lift there's a short walk leading to a staircase at the foot of which is what is left of Mary King's Close—a narrow pavement just 10 feet across. Once a thriving street 100 yards long and packed with houses and shops, there is only 65 feet of it left. The underground tour goes through passages linking to a house in another close. It consists of a large room, 18 feet by 18 feet, with a smaller room partitioned off. As many as 25 members of the same family might have lived here.

The close is thought to be named after Mary, the daughter (alive in 1601) of Alexander King, chief proprietor in the area and Advocate to Mary Queen of Scots. At that time the buildings on either side extended upwards to 5 or 6 storeys.

In 1645 an outbreak of bubonic plague (the Black Death) was rife and supposedly started in Mary King's Close. Local Protestants blamed the outbreak on Mary, who was a Catholic, saying it was God's vengeance upon her. Later they said it was the fault of the Devil. Because of the belief that the disease was carried in the buildings every door and window was bricked up and the close shut down.

A street character of those times was Edinburgh's 'Foule clenger', whose cry 'Bring out your dead' rang out as he collected those felled by the plague.

The area around lay deserted for 110 years before fears of the Black Death were largely forgotten, apart from a brief spell in 1685, when a few families are said to have set up home there when housing was short. The inhabitants of one household—Thomas Coltheart, a law agent from Musselburgh, and his wife—were sitting reading by the fire on their first night of occupation. A strange dimness fell upon the candlelight. The man raised his eyes, and, as he looked at the candle, it turned blue. Six feet away the floating decapitated head of a man with a grey beard looked him straight in the face. He and his wife fainted. When they came to the room was in darkness. The door opened, and in came a hand holding a candle followed by two or three pairs of feet skipping across the floor—the head of a child and a child's arm. They were followed by a spiritual dog, a ghostly cat and other stranger creatures, until the room was filled with apparitions. Then there was a hollow groan and everything vanished. The Colthearts immediately evacuated the place, and it was for ever shut up.

After a century of decay a fire in 1750 reduced the upper part to ruin, and three years later it was incorporated into the Royal Exchange building, later to become the City Chambers.

The close's ghostly reputation is the result of several

hundred years of myth and legend. Parties which visit the close today are reputed to have seen figures in the darkness, also cattle and sheep, and to have heard conversations coming from the room, although nobody was there! At times it has be referred to as the 'Street of Sorrows'.

Allan's Close (within the City Chambers) (269)

Two floors beneath the east wing of the City Chambers are the remains of Allan's Close. The entry from the High Street no longer exists, but a small tablet on the wall indicates the original site. In 1932 the upper storeys were demolished to make way for an extension. But one room survived, and with it a curious tale. This apartment has seen better days, but it has retained interesting features dating back to the 17th century, including the remains of three fireplaces, a built-in cupboard and wall decorations believed to have been there since the 18th century. It is in that room that a young girl is reputed to have been seen sitting on a stove in the corner. Several guided parties to this room have felt a 'presence' there, and a keen Edinburgh historian had a strange experience with a group which included a number of blind people and two guide dogs. The dogs, like most guide dogs, were no problem at all—until they entered the haunted room. One lay against the wall, while the other attempted to pull the person holding the lead out of the room.

Why should two dogs, renowned for their obedience and understanding, react so uncharacteristically? And who is this young girl said to frequent this lonely room down in the bowels of the City Chambers? No-one knows exactly what her story or her background is, but when seen in the past she is reported as having worn a dirty white dress and boots.

Craig's Close (265)

This close took its name from John Craig, wright and burgess. Andrew Hart had premises here, where he brought out an edition of the Bible in 1610. Both Sir Walter Scott and Robert Burns had associations with the close. It had the famous Isle of Man Tavern patronised by Robert Fergusson, Raeburn, Alexander Runciman and Deacon Brodie, and here the *Scotsman* newspaper had its offices. The entry from the High Street no longer exists, having been demolished in 1932 to incorporate it in an extension to the City Chambers; but it is open at the Cockburn Street end.

Old Post Office Close

Since the Post Office moved from Old Post Office Close in the reign of King George I it had several addresses before being housed in its present site (i.e. the GPO) at the end of North Bridge. Like Craig's Close, this no longer exists, having been demolished in 1932 to incorporate it in an extension to the City Chambers; all that remains is a plaque on the wall recording the original position.

Anchor Close (241)

This close, which dated back to 1521, still exists, but the original door was removed from its site and rebuilt in the Canongate in 1937 with the inscription above it: 'O Lord in The is al my Traist'. At one time the close was named from the 'Anchor Tavern in Fuller's Close' kept by George Cumming, where the Lord High Commissioner was long in the habit of holding his levées. Later it was famous when it contained the 'Anchor Tavern Howff of the Crochallan Fencibles', a club attended by Robert Burns. (Fencibles were bands of volunteers raised to resist possible invasion from the Continent as a result of the war in the American Colonies.) The Club got its name from a Gaelic song which the landlord—Daniel (Dawney) Douglas—sang to his customers;

the proper title was 'Cro Chalien' i.e., Colin's Cattle. A round carved oak table made from the rafters of the Crochallan Club rooms can be seen in the writers' museum in Lady Stair's Close

The parents of Sir Walter Scott resided here until 1771, and the close also contained the printing house of William Smellie (printer, naturalist and antiquary) famous for printing Burns's works in 1787 (also where the poet read the proofs) and the first edition of the *Encyclopaedia Britannica* in 1768; Smellie not only printed the first edition, but was also responsible for writing considerable parts of the first three volumes. The close also housed Lord Provost George Drummond, Master of the Merchant Company 1681 (not to be confused with the famous 18th century Lord Provost). At one time the *Scotsman* offices occupied the close until the removal of that newspaper to the North Bridge.

Geddes Entry (233)

This close was formerly called Hutcheson's and Richardson's Close. Named after Robert Geddes, a surgeon of Scotstoun, it dates back to the 17th century. It contained a tavern in which members of the 'Cape Club' met. The poet Robert Fergusson and many other talented men were members of it.

North Foulis Close (229)

It has been suggested that the name of this close was derived from the house, demolished in 1902, occupied by Lady Munro of Fowlis, but it seems to originate from John Foulis (of Colinton), apothecary, owner of a tenement in the close. James Gillespie, of Spylaw, Colinton, had a shop here. He was the founder of James Gillespie's hospital and schools and a tobacco and snuff manufacturer. It was said of him that 'he put his business into other people's noses'!

Old Stamp Office Close (221)

The Countess of Eglinton and her seven beautiful daughters dwelt in a house here. It was a sight worth seeing in those days to observe the whole family setting out of an evening to attend the Dancing Assemblies in Assembly Close, each in her own gilded sedan chair. Allan Ramsay dedicated *The Gentle Shepherd* to her. Later the close housed the 'Fortune's Tavern' (also called 'Ship Tavern' at one time) where the General Assembly's Lord High Commissioner of 1754 held levées. Prince Charlie's Flora Macdonald attended boarding school here. From 1727 to 1753 the Royal Bank was located here and until 1821 the Government Stamp Office was situated here (before transfer to Waterloo Place) and from which it takes its name.

Lyon's Close (215)

Formerly called 'Stalker's Close', and although very old, has no historical significance.

Jackson's Close (209)

Named after several members of a family called Jackson, this close also has no historical background. The classical scholar William Nicol lived here from 1744 to 1794.

Fleshmarket Close (199)

This was formerly called 'Provost's Close', after four-times-Provost, David Aikenhead who lived here in the 17th century, but it was obviously named after the meat market there, which led down to a slaughterhouse at the side of the Nor' Loch. Having been born in Bishop's Close, Henry Dundas, later Viscount Melville (uncrowned 'King of Scotland') lived for some time in the close. William Creech, publisher, started his business in a cellar in this close. The close was divided to allow the construction of Cockburn Street.

(Cockburn Street and North/South Bridge lie here.)

Carrubber's Close.

Carrubber's Close (135)

This is one of the oldest closes in the Old Town to retain its
original name which is reputed to be after William
Carroberos (or Carriberis or de Carabris), a merchant and
magistrate who had his mansion here in 1450, or from one
John Hay of Carruber who stayed nearby. John Spottiswood
(1565–1639), Archbishop of St Andrews and Lord
Chancellor of Scotland, resided here. He crowned King
Charles I at Holyrood in 1633. It was a Jacobite resort from

1688, where members worshipped before the building of Old St Paul's Church.

In 1736 Allan Ramsay had a bookseller's business and later launched a theatre here; it was quickly closed when the godly City magistrates, influenced by the clergy, disapproved and refused it a licence.

The close was also famous in the 1860s for housing the medical dispensary of Sir James Young Simpson, discoverer of the uses of chloroform, whose name was given to Edinburgh's Simpson Memorial Maternity Pavilion. The close also lends its name to the Carrubber's Close Mission, whose church is further down the High Street.

Bishop's Close (129)

Originally known as Edward Nisbet's, James Nisbet's, Patrick Nisbet's, Alexander Lindsay's and Lindsay's Close. Probably built by Bishop Saintserf (or Sydserff), Bishop of Brechin, Galloway and Orkney in the 16th century. Henry Dundas, later Viscount Melville (whose column is in St Andrew Square) was born here in 1742. Robert Burns had lessons here in French from Louis Cauvin, founder of Cauvin's Hospital for Boys, in Duddingston. This area was originally known as Bishop's Land in medieval times, when ecclesiastics built their mansions.

North Gray's Close (125)

The close bore its name prior to 1513. At the foot of the close Old St Paul's Church may be seen. It had connections with Bishop Seabury of America, and with the Jacobite Cause. The name originates from Robert Gray and his father, Alexander Gray, who owned property here, and whose descendants must have lived here for many years.

Morrison's Close (117)

This property was owned by John Morrison (or John Moriesone), merchant, in the early 18th century. At one time it contained interesting old buildings, but these have long since been demolished and replaced. Ruskin's grandfather once lived here.

Bailie Fyfe's Close (107)

Formerly known as Trotter's and Barrie's Close. Originally dates back to 1572. Bailie Gilbert Fyfe, senior merchant, had a house here between 1677 and 1686. Francis Jeffrey, advocate and founder of the *Edinburgh Review*, went to school here in 1781. Nathaniel Gow, son of Neil Gow, taught violin and piano in the close. Many legal, literary and musical people lived here through the ages. The crest over the entrance bears the initials 'I.P—M.H.'. The Parley, Yorkshire, Arms, impaled with those of Hay, at one time adorned the doorway of a residence in the close.

Paisley Close (101)

This close was originally owned by George Henderson of Fordell, who sold the land to Henry Paislie in 1711. Wine

Crest over the entrance to Bailie Fyfe's close.

Carving over the entrance to Paisley Close.

and tea merchant, Sir William Fettes, founder of Fettes College, had a shop here. The close rose to fame on 24 November 1861 when disaster struck. The 250-year-old tenement in an adjacent close (Bailie Fyfe's Close) collapsed, killing 35 inhabitants. Workmen clearing the debris heard a voice calling out, 'Heave awa' lads, ah'm no' deid yet'. It came from a young lad, believed to be one, Joseph McIver, trapped in the rubble, calling out words of encouragement to his rescuers. When the tenement was rebuilt the young boy's face was carved into the sculptured lintel above the door as a memorial in Paisley Close along with a slightly anglicized version of his cry, 'Heave away chaps, I'm not dead yet'. Though the city was not responsible for erecting the inscription the assistant archivist has said that it was the original put up in 1862 at the rebuilding of the collapsed building. The builders commissioned a local stonemason, Robert Paterson, to carry out the work. The reason for the anglicizing of the words is unclear. The common version of the words is that accepted by contemporary writings; they could have been passed on wrongly by the builder, or perhaps, as is more likely, it was considered more genteel, since middle-class Edinburgh at that time still clung to its conservative 'North British' image which had been so carefully nurtured earlier in the century by people like Sir Walter Scott. Long after the tragedy the close was sometimes referred to as 'Heave Awa' Land' and the rescued boy was believed to have lived to a good age.

As a result of this tragedy the overcrowding and appalling conditions under which people lived were highlighted and the office of Medical Officer of Health was created. Dr (later Sir) Henry D. Littlejohn was appointed to the post.

Chalmer's Close (81)

This gives access to Holy Trinity Church Hall, normally called Trinity College Apse, one of the saddest medieval remains in Edinburgh. The original Trinity Church, built in the 15th century, was an exquisite piece of Gothic architecture, but was demolished in the 19th century to make room for the railway to Waverley. Though the stones were carefully numbered and stored on the Calton Hill for re-erection on the present site, pilfering to mend garden walls etc, depleted the stock so much that only the present hall could be put together in 1852 using masonry from the original choir and apse. Visitors can now test their skills at the Brass

TRINITY COLLEGE
·CHURCH·

MAP SHOWING ORIGINAL AND SUBSEQUENT LOCATION of TRINITY COLLEGE CHURCH

TRINITY COLLEGE CHURCH, JUST BEFORE ITS DEMOLITION IN 1848, SHOWING WAGONS OF THE NORTH BRITISH RAILWAY COMPANY. PHOTOGRAPH BY ROSS AND THOMSON. Copyright reserved. Reproduced by gracious permission of H.M. The Queen.

DESTRUCTION, LITIGATION AND PARTIAL RE-ERECTION

*I*n 1845 Trinity College Church and Hospital were sold to the North British Railway Company, who wished to use the site for the extension of Waverly Station. At first it was agreed that the company would have to acquire a site and rebuild the church, but the Town Council later accepted the sum of £16,371/9s/6d in return for discharging the company from its obligation. The hospital was demolished in 1845, and the church in 1848, but pressure from antiquarians persuaded the council to provide for the possibility of rebuilding the church elsewhere. Measured drawings were made, and all the building stones were individually numbered before demolition took place.

A search was made beneath the church for the grave of Mary of Gueldres, and remains believed to be those of the Queen were removed and reinterred at Holyrood Chapel, but the discovery shortly afterwards of a second female burial gave rise to disputes as to whether a mistake had been made.

For almost a quarter of a century the stones of Trinity College Church lay on the slopes of Calton Hill, while a series of legal actions ensued over

whether it should be rebuilt, on which site, and how much money should be spent. Eventually it was decided that only £7000 should be devoted to the building of a new church in the vicinity, and that the remainder of the money received from the railway company should be given to the funds of Trinity Hospital. The sum allocated was far too small for the old church to be rebuilt, and in any case many of the stones had been stolen or damaged, so a new church was erected on the south side of Jeffrey Street, with an apsidal hall at the south end built from as many as possible of the stones from the old church. This is the building in which you are now standing. The new church opened for worship in 1877.

TRINITY APSE, VIEW FROM THE NORTH IMMEDIATELY AFTER DEMOLITION OF THE 19TH CENTURY CHURCH. Photograph by R.A. Hill

The Victorian church was sold in 1959 and demolished shortly afterwards, leaving the rebuilt apse standing on its own. It passed into the ownership of Edinburgh Corporation, who restored it and converted it for use as a newspaper reading room. It served this purpose from 1965 to 1974, and after a short period of disuse it then served as a museum store until 1986. It was reopened to the public shortly afterwards.

A descriptive notice inside Trinity college Apse within Chalmer's Close showing the original Church before its demolition in 1848.

Rubbing Centre, housed within the building, and well worth a visit.

The close name is derived from Patrick Chalmers, belt maker, who owned a tenement here; he was Captain in the

Trained Bands 1682 and probably of the 'Green and Reid' in 1685. The close has at other times been called Chamber's, Dunsyre's and Boyd's Close, and was once the residence of Lord Jeffrey's grandfather.

Monteith's Close (61)

Formerly Fleming's Close. None of the old buildings which dated from 1562 exist, and this is another close of no historical interest. The older name was derived from Patrick Fleeming, who owned property in the High Street, also a 'tinnice court' (tennis!).

Trunk's Close (55)

The name comes from the Aberdeenshire family, Turings of Foveran, who stayed in a house on the west side about 1529. Lord Heathfield, son of Sir Gilbert Elliot of Stobs, and hero of the Siege of Gibraltar, is believed to have resided here while attending school in Edinburgh. In 1802 the *Edinburgh Review* was published here.

Moubray House—see Page 78

Hope's Court

This property was owned by a Dr Archibald Hope before it was acquired by Baron John Maule in 1766, one of the Barons of the Court of the Exchequer in Scotland. The court is closed behind a small locked door in a corner below John Knox house and can be easily overlooked.

John Knox House—see Page 78
Netherbow Port—see Page 78

Baron Maule's Close (13)

Called after Henry Maule of Kellie, brother of the Earl of Panmure. His son, John Maule of Inverkeilor, advocate, was appointed a Baron of the Court of Exchequer in 1748. In 1624 the close was called Bassendyne's, after Thomas Bassendyne, printer.

Canongate

(Jeffrey Street and Cranston Street lie here).

Morocco Land (273)

Was in a desolate state before it was rebuilt in the 1950s,
complete with the mysterious figure of a Moor high up on
the outside of the building over-looking the street. Several
legends surround this figure. One has it that early in the 17th
century Andrew Gray (a local 'Dick Whittington'), a student
and younger son of a noble family, was imprisoned and
sentenced to death following a disturbance outside the Lord
Provost's office. He escaped to sea and rose to a top post in
the household of the Emperor of Morocco, making his
fortune. He is reputed to have returned to Edinburgh in 1645
in disguise. Discovering that the Provost's daughter (his
cousin) was suffering from the plague, which raged in the
town, he cured her with an elixir. Legend has it that he
married her and set up home in Morocco Land, having the
life-sized effigy of a Moor erected on the outside (directly
above Mid Common Close). Other tales have it that the
Provost's daughter was in the harem of the ruler of Morocco,
and that her brother used his influence to make a fortune
trading with that country. In gratitude he had the figure
placed on the building. Whatever the reason it is a curious
tourist attraction.

Mid Common Close (269)

Among others, this close gave access to the school or High
School of the Canongate, not to be confused with the old
Royal High School. In the 19th century it was called
'Vietche's Close' after John Veitch, burgess, who built a
tenement here, later owned by Thomas Veitch, surgeon. It
is of no historical interest.

(New Street lies here).

Sculptured shield of an open Bible above the doorway of 'Bible land'.

Bible Land (185)

Formerly Shoemaker's or Land's Close). Was called by its present name on account of the sculptured shield over the doorway, showing an open Bible on which is quoted the first verse of the old Scottish Metrical Version of Psalm 133. Above the Bible are the Shoemakers' Arms—the crown and rounding knife or paring knife of King St Crispin, patron saint of shoemakers or Cordiners of the Canongate:

1677—Behold how good a thing it is and how becoming well,
Together such as Brethren are in Unity to Dwell.?
'It is an honour for men to cease from strife'.

Gladstone Court (181)

Formerly Bowling Green Close

Has no historical interest, apart from the fact that it was re-named in honour of W.E. Gladstone MP, former Prime Minister. It did originally have a bowling green overlooked by prisoners in the Tolbooth Jail. In later years an asylum (Magdalene Asylum) was built on the green, but in 1865 this was removed to Dalry.

Canongate Tolbooth—see Page 81

Old Tolbooth Wynd (165)

This close, built in 1591, takes its name from the Auld Tolbuith of the Canongate, the entrance to it being a vaulted pend under the Tolbooth itself. The Tolbooth was originally the booth in which the tolls were paid. It was the council chambers of the old Burgh of Canongate, a police court, and latterly a prison. It is recognised by its turreted steeple and large clock dating from 1879. Is now a museum telling 'The People's Story' and is just what the name implies—using oral history, reminiscence and written sources. The displays have been based on first hand accounts of Edinburgh life, work and pastimes from the late 18th Century to the present day. It is about brewing, printing, shipbuilding, biscuit and confectionery manufacture, banking, retailing and domestic service. The museum is filled with the sounds, sights and smells of life in the past—a prison cell, town crier, cooper's workshop, draper's shop, fishwife, servant at work, tramcar 'clippie', 1940's kitchen, 'steamie', pub and tearoom.

Canongate Church—see Page 82

Dunbar's Close (137)

In a quiet secluded garden off the Canongate lies Dunbar's Close Garden, sometimes called 'The Mushroom Garden'.

Old Tolbooth Wynd and clock tower of Canongate Tolbooth looking westwards up the Royal Mile, and the entrance to 'The People's Story'.

Laid out in the character of an Edinburgh 17th-century garden and donated by the Mushroom Trust to the City of Edinburgh, it is a delightful spot only a step away from the busy thoroughfare. There one has time to relax on the wooden or stone benches and view rows of fruit trees, lavender plants, bushes, carnations and an assortment of flowers.

Here a Mrs Love had an oyster cellar below Canongate Church. When Robert Burns was in town he would frequent

Plaque inside Dunbar's close Garden, also showing 'Patrick Geddes Heritage Trail' plaque.

the cellar and watch ladies of fashion wearing masks 'eating oysters and drinking porter'. The tenements on both sides of the close belonged to David Dunbar, writer, in 1773, who gave his name to the close.

Panmure Close (129)

At one time called McKell's Close. Here the Jacobite Earl of Panmure, had his town house and garden in the mid-eighteenth century. It was called after Panmure House, built in 1691, and later occupied by the Countess of Aberdeen until 1778. Her occupancy was followed by that of Adam Smith, Commissioner of the Customs, and author of *The Wealth of Nations*, who lived there from 1778 to 1790. In his time the house must have seen the most intellectual company in Scotland. The close is now gated and leads to flats and garden ground.

Entrance to Panmure Close in the Canongate.

Little Lochend Close (115) & Lochend Close. (105)

These buildings probably date back to the 17th century and appear to be connected with William Ferguson of Lochend, Restalrig, who owned property here, and latterly to John Ferguson, tanner and burgess. They possibly obtained their names from a village of this name at Restalrig. Apart from this they apparently have no historical background.

Reid's Court (95)

Also known as Blyth's Close. Built about 1690 but named after an 18th-century family called Reid, who were coachmakers and owned the site. Was at various times called a yard, a coach-yard and a close. Was the Manse of the Canongate until 1832, and again from 1958 to the present time.

Campbell's Close (87)

Originally called Rae's Close. Several notable people had their residences here, among them Arthur Ross, Archbishop of St Andrews, and Colonel George Douglas, later 13th Earl of Morton, and his son James, 14th Earl. The close was originally named after a meal merchant, George Campbell, Bailie of the Canongate, who owned property there.

Brown's Close (Golfer's Land) (81/79)

Formerly called Sommerville's Close, after John Sommerville, gunsmith. It is, however, named after Joseph Brown, baxter, merchant and Burgess of Edinburgh who acquired the tenement and close which was at the time called Paterson's Land and Close.

The tenement known as Golfer's Land stood on this site. The story goes that in the 17th century it was built by Bailie John Paterson (a shoemaker and maker of leather golf balls) with his share of the stakes from a golf match on Leith Links when at the time he was a poor shoemaker in the Canongate. Two English noblemen at Holyrood had been in discussion with the Duke of York (later James VII) as to the native country of golf, insisting it was an English game. In order to prove their expertise they staked their statements on the result of a match between themselves and the Duke with any Scotsman he might select to partner him. After very careful

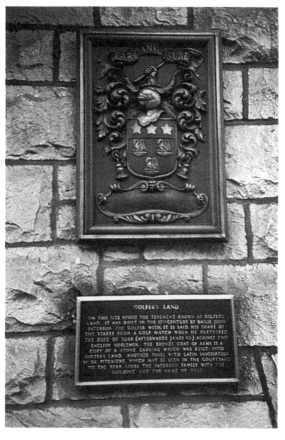

Bronze coat of arms outside Golfer's Land and entrance to Brown's Close.

enquiry he chose John Paterson, who, he was informed, was descended from a long line of golfers. The English noblemen were beaten, the Duke of York had the success of the argument, and Paterson was rewarded with the stakes played for. He in turn is reputed to have built the house in the Canongate.

A bronze coat of arms (Paterson's) is displayed on the

outside of the building. It is a copy of a stone carving which was built into Golfer's Land, and displays a dexter hand grasping a golf club over a knight's helmet with the motto, dear to all golfers, 'Far and Sure'. Below the helmet are three five-pointed stars (or mullets) and three pelicans.

In another part of the building is a panel with a Latin inscription by Dr Archibald Pitcairne, poet and wit, which links the Paterson family with the building and the name of golf. It reads:

> CUM VICTOR LUDO SCOTIS QUI PROPRIUS, ESSET,
> TER TRES VICTORES POST REMEDITOS AVOS
> PATERSONUS, HUMO TUNC EDUCEBAT IN ALTUM
> HANC, QUAE VICTORES TOT TULET UNA DOMUM
> I HATE NO PERSON.

This is referred to in the *Edinburgh Magazine & Review* for 1774, and literally translated means: 'In the year when Paterson won the prize in golfing, a game peculiar to the Scots, in which his ancestors had nine times won the same honour, he then raised this mansion, a victory more honourable than all the rest'. The English words, 'I hate no person' are an anagram of John Patersone!

However there would appear to be some doubt as to the authenticity of these events, which seem to have taken place about 1681, since Paterson's grandfather acquired the building in 1601 and it had therefore been in the family long before the game of golf was played.

In his old 19th-century book *Traditions of Edinburgh* Robert Chambers states:

> It must be admitted there is some uncertainty about this tale. The house, the inscriptions and arms only indicate that Paterson built the house after being a victor at golf and that Dr Pitcairne had a hand in decorating it. It might have been expected that if Paterson had been enriched by a match in which he was connected with the Duke of York, a Jacobite like Pitcairne would have made a distinct allusion to the circumstances. The

tradition, never-the-less, seems too curious to be entirely overlooked.

The truth of the legend must therefore be left to the visitor's imagination. Paterson sold the property to either John Brown, gardener, or Joseph Brown merchant and Burgess of Edinburgh.

Near Golfer's Land and Galloway's Entry stood Jenny Ha's Tavern or Change House. Old taverns were known by their landlords' names—this one was called after Janet Hall.

The old law of 1699 forbidding employment of women in taverns, cellars and drinking shops as being 'a great snare to the Youth and Occasion for Loudness and Debauchery' had been challenged and severed. The feminine tasks and often motherly kindness made these taverns memorable throughout the years.

The Tavern stood on this site near the foot of the Canongate from 1600 to 1857 and was frequented by John Gay (author of *The Beggars Opera*) in 1729, and by fellow poet Allan Ramsay; it was also a tavern favoured by Jacobites and Episcopalian Clergy.

Forsyth's Close (Gloucester Gate) (57)

Named after Alexander Forsyth in 1719, who was coachmaker and Burgess of Edinburgh. To those who travelled to London by stage-coach Forsyth's stables and coach houses were nearby. The close is an entry to Whiteford House.

Whiteford (or Whitefoord) House (within Galloway's Entry) (53)

It occupies the site of the Earl of Winton's town mansion in which Lord Darnley stayed briefly prior to his marriage to Mary Queen of Scots. It was better known as My Lord Seytoun's Lugeing (lodging) in the Canongate (referred to in Sir Walter Scott's *The Abbot* Vol. 1 Chapter 18, published in 1820 as part of the Waverley Novel series). George Seton, the 5th Lord Seton, acted as host to Mary, Queen of Scots, of whom he was a loyal supporter. After Winton Mansion was demolished Sir John Whiteford of Ballochmyle (died 1803) built the present house from whom it takes its name. It is now home to many ex-soldier, sailor and air force veterans. Callender's Entry was in this vicinity but no longer exists, although Callender House, built mid-18th-century, still exists, joined to Whiteford House. The tavern or ale-house, mentioned under Brown's Close and frequented by Gay and Ramsay, was in Callender's Entry.

White Horse Close (31)

(Formerly Davidson's Close and Merchant Laurence Ord's Close) It bears the false date 1523, the real date being either 1603 or 1623, although an inn probably stood here earlier on the same site. It was used as a Royal Mews in the 16th century and in 1623 a merchant, Laurence Ord, rebuilt the existing tenement as court, hayloft, and houses, also an inn (the White Horse Inn) and coaching stables, having a large entry gate. It was named after Mary, Queen of Scots' white

Picturesque and much photographed and sketched White Horse Close, Canongate.

palfrey and *not* after the White Horse of Hanover. In 1639 Charles I met Scots nobles here for a conference.

The stables of Holyroodhouse are thought to have been situated here before the Inn became the terminus for stage-coaches to Newcastle and London. In 1754 a stage-coach leaving for London took eight days to the journey, travellers being allowed 14 lbs of luggage. Scotland Yard, home of London's police, got its name because it was the London terminus for the coaches from Edinburgh. Jacobite officers used the Inn as HQ in the 1745 rebellion while Prince Charles Edward Stuart was resident in Holyrood Palace.

William Dick, born in 1793, who founded the Royal (Dick) School of Veterinary Studies in 1823 was the son of an Edinburgh blacksmith and at one time resided in the close.

It was restored and given a new frontage in 1965 and now sports modern houses and a picturesque courtyard of old world character much visited, photographed, sketched and admired by tourists.

It has in turn given it's name to a well known brand of whisky!

———————

WE HAVE NOW REACHED ABBEY STRAND AND THE ENTRANCE TO HOLYROOD PALACE. BY CROSSING TO THE SOUTH SIDE OF THE CANONGATE, HOWEVER VISITORS CAN NOW RETRACE THEIR STEPS BY ASCENDING THE ROYAL MILE ON THAT SIDE OF THE STREET AND VISITING AND READING ABOUT THE FOLLOWING CLOSES, ETC.

Closes etc., In the South Side of the Royal Mile

Canongate

Vallence's Entry (72)

Known at times as Vallene's or Vallen's Close and Valentine's Entry, it was named after Adam Vallange in 1775, barber and possibly wigmaker, but otherwise is of no historic interest.

(Next to the entry is Queensberry House built in 1634 and occupied by the Duke of Queensberry and his heirs between 1681 and 1801. Later it was used as barracks then a hospital and latterly a hospital for the elderly.) See also entry in page 83.

Reid's Close (80)

This close takes its name from Andrew Reid, maltster and Bailie in 1770, who succeeded the occupation by the Earls of Aberdeen. It was also the residence of Sir John Nisbet of Dirleton (1609–87) an unpopular Lord Advocate of Charles II, and contained the town house of the Earl of Haddington in the late 17th century. Sir John Nisbet's house was rebuilt in the 20th century as a replica of the original next to the Royal Mile School (formerly Milton House school). The original lintels were built in above the door part of which read 'Blissit be God in all his giftis.'

Bull's Close (100)

Named after Robert Bull who was a wright and Burgess of Edinburgh in 1701. The close has also been called May Drummond's and Dr Drummond's Close, Ford's Row and Lamont's Land. The name May or Marion or Marianna Drummond relates to the daughter of George Drummond, one-time Lord Provost of Edinburgh. She was known as the

Old doorway removed from Anchor Close in the High Street in 1932 and re-sited here in the Canongate in 1937.

'Preaching Quakeress', celebrated by Pope, Spence and others. Old buildings which once stood on this site were connected with the Blackfriars Monastery. Over the close entrance is an inscribed tablet, a relic from an old tenement, which reads:

AUX ILIUM A DNO 1586—IV.
MY HELP IS OF YE L(ORD)—HE.

(By pausing at ACHESON HOUSE, next to Huntly House, the visitor will see the old original doorway taken from Anchor Close at 241 High Street in 1932 and rebuilt here in 1937.)

Acheson House & Huntly House—see Pages 83–84

Bakehouse Close (146)

This close was formerly known as Huntly Close, Cordiner's Close or Hammermen's Close (i.e. Headquarters of the metal workers).

Entrance to Bakehouse Close—note the thickness of the wall!

It is not known who built it, but the archway dates from 1570 and relates to the joining of three houses into one. At the east end of an old mansion house—Huntly House—the close gave access to every part of the house as there was no entrance from the street. The inhabitants in those far off days must therefore have had a feeling of security against intruders when the gateway was closed.

Initially local talk must have been against the construction of such a mansion, causing the building to be nicknamed the 'Speaking House', when the owner displayed a tablet over the ground floor which read—'HODIE MIHI: CRAS TIBI. CUR IGITUR CURAS?' and which when translated read—

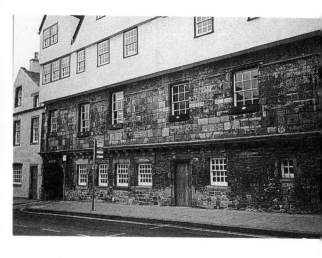

Huntly House Museum and entrance to Bakehouse Close to the left of the photograph, also the inscribed Latin tablets replaced on the outside of the building in 1932.

'I am the happy man today; your turn may come tomorrow. Why then should you repine?'

As the building was added to, public concern became more bitter. This caused the owner to erect a second tablet in defiance—'UT TU LINGUAE TUAE, SIC EGO MEAR(UM) AURIU(M), DOMINUS SUM'—(or 'As thou of thy tongue, so I of my ears am Lord').

Later as pressure slackened he appeared to mellow to a religious theme—CONSTANTI PERTORI RES MORTALIUM UMBRA—('To the constant heart temporal things are but a shadow') with an emblem of Christian hope of Resurrection, and finally—'SPES ALTERA VITAE'—(with ears of wheat emerging from a handful of bones)—'Another hope of Life'.

These inscribed tablets were later removed to inside the

buildings and replaced in 1932 by 'ANTIQUA TAMEN T.B.W.' (for Sir Thomas B Whitson, Lord Provost).

The Dowager Duchess of Gordon occupied a flat in Huntly House in 1753, giving her name to it.

The current name comes from the bakehouse and property on the west side of it taken over in 1832 by the Guild of the Incorporation of Bakers of the Canongate. In it were the quarters of the bakers and hammermen as well as the residence of the Acheson family who formed the household staff of James VI and Charles I.

Records from 1851 indicate that 230 people lived in the close.

Huntly House is now a principal City Museum, having been purchased in 1924.

Sugarhouse Close (160)

Originally owned by the Earl of Dunkeld. So named because of an old sugar refinery—'The Sugar Workhouse'—here in 1752 but it was burned down in 1800. It must have been restored however, for the firm of David Jardine & Co., sugar refiners, conducted business here in 1824 as the Edinburgh Sugar House.

St John's Pend (188)

The Knights of St John had their house in this district thus giving it the name. The entrance to the street was built about 1768. Houses were occupied by famous families and occasionally Tobias Smollett (1721–1771) stayed here with his sister, Mrs. Telfer. He was a doctor, but made his name as a novelist and editor of various magazines and historical works, *Humphrey Clinker* being the best-known. Robert Burns was made Poet Laureate in Freemasons' Lodge Canongate Kilwinning No. 2 here in 1787.

It seems that land here belonged to various religious denominations subject to the Canons of Holyrood. The

**The Priory of Scotland of the Most Venerable Order of St
John within St John's Pend showing the Maltese Cross of
the Order.**

Knights were members of landowning families who built
houses close to the Palace of Holyrood. The Priory of
Scotland of the Most Venerable Order of St John still exists
in St John Street and is mainly concerned with fund raising
for charity. Displayed above the door is the Maltese Cross of
the Order—also on the gate. No attempt was made to
protect this part of Edinburgh by a wall.

Moray House—see Page 84

Old Playhouse Close (196)

An old 16th-century close led to the first of Edinburgh's
theatres and hall which lay between this and Playhouse Close.
The foundation stone of the theatre called the 'Canongate
Theatre' was laid in 1746 by John Ryan of London's Covent
garden, an actor of some distinction. From 1747 to 1786
famous actors, actresses and singers performed here. The
Rev. John Home's tragedy *Douglas* was first staged here in
1756, much to the outrage of the Church of Scotland, who by

A painted Maltese Cross of the Order of St John on the roadway of the Canongate just below Old Playhouse Close.

tradition opposed all theatre, and this eventually led to his resignation from the ministry. Tobias Smollett lived here in 1766, gathering material for his *Humphrey Clinker*. A Maltese Cross of the Order of St John is painted on the roadway just below this close (see information under St John's Pend)

A plaque on the wall nearby states:-

'The Cross on the roadway marks the site of the original standing cross of St John which was on the boundary between Edinburgh and the Burgh of Canongate. The Ancient Order of St John is thought to have owned land and property next to the cross during the Middle Ages.

The Cross was set in place during 1987 by the Venerable Order of St John of Jerusalem to mark the 40th anniversary of the Re-establishment of the Order in Scotland.'

Chessel's Court (240)

Was said to have been the finest example of mansion flats in the Old Town built in 1748 by Archibald Chessel, a wright and merchant.

Chessel's Court in the Canongate—where Deacon Brodie met his downfall.

In 1963 the buildings were completely restored and renovated, the upper storeys of the building fronting the Canongate being supported on columns, giving an open aspect of the court from the main street, with a fine arcade.

This close rose to fame in 1788 when the infamous Deacon Brodie broke into the General Excise office here, thus leading to his downfall—(see the story as told in 'Brodie's Close').

Gibb's Close (250)

Charles, 4th Earl of Traquair, built and lived in a high tenement here in 1700 with his twin daughters. Later Robert Gibb, coachbuilder, lived here and gave his name to the close which gained fame in the 19th century when one of Burke and Hare's victims met her death in one of the houses.

Gullan's Close (264)

Has had several names—Gullon's from James Gullan, sta-
bler, Haliburton's and Cant's Close. The close is of no
historical interest; it leads to the Cowgate and branches into
St Mary's Street

(St Mary's Street lies here).

High Street

World's End Close (10)

The last close in the High Street before the old City gates so
called because it was outside the protection of the walls.
There was once an old fishmarket here. The original name
was probably Swift's Close after John Swift (or Swyft) in
1427. It was later called Stanfield's Close after Sir James
Stanfield of Amisfield whose tragic death by drowning in
1687 was shrouded in mystery when his body was disinterred
and it was discovered he had been strangled. His son Philip
was executed having been proved guilty of the murder by
the 'ordeal of blood' after a trial in which the evidence was
based on the science of demonology and tortured witnesses.
At the hanging the drop on the gibbet did not kill Stanfield
at first go, and the executioner had to take over and finish
the job with his bare hands—his tongue was then cut out, his
hand severed, and his head spiked.

Tweeddale Court (14)

Formerly John Laing's Close—he was Keeper of the
Signet—Alexander Young's Close; James Brown's Close
and Marquis of Tweeddale's Close).

Dates from 1589 and was at one time occupied by Sir
William Bruce of Balcaskie, architect of Holyrood Palace,
who died in 1710. It contained the town residence of Hay,
Marquis of Tweeddale, having at one time a terraced garden
with elm trees extending to the Cowgate and described by

Defoe as one of the most princely buildings in Edinburgh. It was occupied by various members of the Tweeddale clan until 1790, when it was sold to the British Linen Co. who made it their headquarters until 1808. The house was then bought by Cowan, paper-maker, and then in 1817 by Oliver & Boyd, whose representatives Grant and Thin, carried on the publishing business under the old name.

In 1806 a tragedy occurred when William Begbie, a porter for the British Linen Co, was fatally stabbed in a passage leading to the courtyard and robbed of a parcel containing £4,392 in notes. The identity of the ruffian who committed the murder was not confirmed until the eve of his execution for another crime.

The Court houses the Scottish Poetry Library and the last sedan chair garage in Edinburgh.

Fountain Close (22)

The name of this close is derived from the fountain or street well which stood opposite the close, until in 1813 it was removed further up to where the street was wider. It was here in 1574 that Thomas Bassendyne, printer, produced the earliest edition of the New Testament Bible printed in Scotland. Here also the publishers, Oliver & Boyd, founded in 1778, occupied a portion of the Hall of the Royal College of Physicians, later converted to an Episcopal Church and then to a Roman Catholic Church.

At times it was known as Moubray's, Stevenson's, Bassendene's, Fullerton's, John Baxton's, and Collington's Close—the latter after Sir James Foulis. It now houses the Saltire Society.

Hyndford's Close (34)

Like Fountain Close above, this close also had an older name of Collingtoun's Close.

For many a year the 17th-century mansion of the

Carmichaels, Earls of Hyndford, stood in this close. The Earl of Selkirk lived here and it was later occupied by Professor Daniel Rutherford, inventor of the gas lamp and maternal grandfather of Sir Walter Scott, who, as a boy, was a frequent visitor. The Duchess of Gordon, friend of Robert Burns and a staunch Jacobite, resided here as a young girl and had a favourite pastime of riding down the street on a pig! The Lodge of St David stood in this close and in 1801 Sir Walter Scott was made a mason here.

Latterly it has been the site of the Museum of Childhood, housing a collection of Victorian, Edwardian and later period toys, games & children's books.

South Gray's Close (40)

As far back as 1512 the name of the close referred to John Gray, Burgess, and it was formerly part of the possessions of the Grey Friars which may suggest another origin of the name. At one time it was called Mint Close and Coyne-House Close because it housed Scotland's Royal Mint from 1574 until 1877, but coins ceased to be minted there in 1709 although officials of the mint continued to dwell in houses there.

The 11th Earl of Buchan had a town house here, and his two sons were born here—one, Henry Erskine (1746–1817), became Dean of the Faculty of Advocates and Lord Advocate, and the other, Thomas Erskine (1750–1823), was later Lord Chancellor of Great Britain. Other houses in the close were owned by the Wedderburns of Gosford, the Earl of Rosslyn, and the Earls of Hyndford and Selkirk.

Part of the old City wall, dating from 1450, was reputed to be in part of this close. St Patrick's Catholic Church is now here. In 1847 a school known as the United Industrial School with 50 children attending was opened here.

Museum of Childhood—see Page 84.

Toddrick's Wynd

Dates back to 1456. It had a special place in history, because when Queen Mary and her train were coming up the wynd, after visiting Darnley at Kirk o' Field on 9 February 1567, James Hepburn, Earl of Bothwell, and his accomplices were stealing down this narrow alley with the gunpowder and other materials for Darnley's assassination.

In 1592 it belonged to Archibald Todrig, Bailie, Baker and Burgess, when it was known as Todrig's Close. The wynd was one of the 'bounds' of the Town Guard in 1685

(Blackfriars Street lies here)

Melrose Close (66)

Now incorporated within the Scandic Hotel, it takes it's name from the lodging of Andrew Durie, Abbot, 1526, who died in 1588, and from whom it took also the longer name of the Abbot of Melrose Close. The lodging was later occupied by Lord Strichen in the mid-1700s.

Cant's Close (70)

Now incorporated within the Scandic Hotel. Named after the owners of Priestfield (or Prestonfield) and of St Giles' Grange who had a town house here. The close ran down to the Cowgate.

In early times, about 1449, it was occupied by ecclesiastical buildings, and later, in 1514, was known as Alexander Cant's Close. The fore-land of olden times at the head of the close was the town-lodging of the Provost of the Collegiate Church of Crichton.

Dickson's Close (80)

Now incorporated within the Scandic Hotel. (Previously known as Bruce's, Haliburton's, Aikman's and Dixon's Close)

It is a recent revival of an old close firstly demolished for

Dickson's Close now incorporated in the Scandic Hotel.

more modern buildings, e.g. Grant's Furniture Store which, in 1970, was demolished due to subsidence, and more recently being incorporated into the Scandic Hotel.

John Dickson and his son Thomas lived here about 1750. At one time it ran down to the Cowgate and housed the Royal College of Surgeons.

In 1773 the occupants of this land were 'graded'. First

floor—fishmonger; 2nd floor—lodging house of good repute; 3rd floor—house of the Dowager Countess of Balcarres; 4th floor—house of a gentle lady; 5th floor—milliners and mantua or mantie makers (i.e. dressmakers); and 6th floor—a variety of tailors and other tradesmen.

It is interesting to note that until the 19th century most shops had a signboard indicating the kind of goods sold, e.g. the upholsterer adopted the 'golden sofa'; the hosier—the 'woolpack'; the barber—a red and white pole with bleeding dish; the fishmonger—a fish with scales and fins; the druggist—a mortar and pestle. Many of these signs still exist in the city today

(Niddry Street, Tron Church and Hunter Square lie here). *Tron Kirk*—see page 85.

Stevenlaw's Close (132)

The name of this close is taken from Steven Law (or Loch, glazier, or Steivin or Stewin Law, flesher) a supporter of Queen Mary during the Civil War of 1571.

In the close was a Roman Catholic Chapel in which Prince Charles Edward worshipped frequently.

In 1786/7 Robert Burns called here on Allan Masterton, High School writing-master.

New Assembly Close (142)

Originally housed the mansion of John Murray of Blackbarony, about 1580, father of Sir Gideon Murray, the 1st Lord Elibank. The close leads to New Assemblies Hall, an attractive Georgian building built by Gillespie Graham. In turn it had accommodated public dances ('dancing Assemblies Hall' 1766–84), the King's Arms Tavern, the Highland Society, a Masonic Lodge, The Commercial Bank of Scotland (from 1814 to 1847), the Centre for the Royal Scottish Society for the Prevention of Cruelty to Children, the Children's Shelter, and the Edinburgh Wax Museum. It now belongs to the Faculty of Advocates.

Bell's Wynd (146)

This wynd took its name from John Bell who was a brewer here in 1529. Some records indicate that, like New Assembly Close at (142), this wynd was also occupied by the Commercial Bank of Scotland, the King's Arms Tavern, the Highland Society and the Children's Shelter, and dancing was held in the New Assembly Rooms—possibly because of the proximity of the close to the wynd.

After John Bell it came into the possession of the Bishop of Dunkeld.

A strange tale is told about this wynd:

A George Gourlay had lived with his wife on the second floor for a number of years. The house below had lain empty for 21 years. Before they were married George's wife had lived in the house below but refused to talk about it. To him it was shrouded in mystery and was to prove to be one of the most sinister and ghostly places in the Old Town. George, a blacksmith and locksmith to trade, his curiosity aroused over the years, decided one night to investigate. With the keys of his trade and a candle he let himself into the strange house and entered the kitchen.

There he found plates all ready to be served to the dining room, which was set for two people and where indications of uneaten food and drink were visible. On entering the bedroom he disturbed a ghostly figure which silently slid by him. On the four poster bed he glanced at a skeleton which appeared to stare at him.

Returning hurriedly to his own apartment he did not tell his wife of his experience, but by coincidence, two days later an old man knocked on his door and spoke about his find as though he was aware of the circumstances. It transpired he had been the owner of the sinister house and the story goes he had returned unexpectedly one night to find his wife with another man. In a fit of rage he killed them both and his servant (now Mr Gourlay's wife) while preparing a meal had witnessed the ghastly scene.

The man paid her ten guineas never to mention the sordid matter. He then closed up the house and disappeared.

Twenty-one years later the affair was reported to the Fiscal who was very lenient in his dealing with the case by merely making the man bury his wife. His comment was that the man's conscience had paid highly over the years for his deed.

Burnet's Close (156)

In 1564 this close was called Johnston's Close after Sir William Johnston who was associated with it; he started the map making firm of W.& A.K. Johnston in the close. (They produced their famous plan of Edinburgh and Leith in 1851.)

After Johnston a Samuel Burnet lived here in 1591; he was a wealthy brewer, merchant, burgess and guild brother, and his name is still associated with the close. Here also stood the town house of Lord Auchinleck, Scots judge, and father of James Boswell, the biographer of Dr Samuel Johnson.

The first edition of *The Scots Magazine* was published in a building in the close in 1739; the building was burned down in 1824.

Covenant Close (162)

In a house in this close in 1638 lay, for signature, one of the copies of the National Covenant being approved at Greyfriar's Church; it was a protest by citizens against Charles I's attempt to establish Episcopacy in Scotland.

Lord Braxfield, Lord Justice-Clerk from 1780 to 1799, resided for a while here. He was noted for his harshness towards political offenders and as a result Robert Louis Stevenson's *Weir of Hermiston* was based on him.

Covenant House was built by James Hamilton, wealthy wright and burgess.

Old Assembly Close (172)

Clement Little, advocate and founder of the University Library, lived here in the 16th century. His brother, William, Provost of Edinburgh in 1585, also lived in the

Entrance to Burnet's Close in the High Street.

close. Both were sons of an Edinburgh cloth and wool merchant.

The close was originally called Little's Close after the brothers; it was also called Durie's Close at one time, after Lord Durie, another former resident.

Between 1720 and 1766 dancing assemblies were held in the Hall hence the current name of the close. George Heriot's bequest funded one of the offshoots of Heriot's main school here before the days of elementary education. Edinburgh's most disastrous fire broke out on a November night in 1824 in a large house in the close. All the buildings except one on the south side of the High Street between this close and Parliament Square were destroyed, including the steeple of the Tron Church.

Within the close the Mackenzie Building was restored in 1993 by the Faculty of Advocates in Commemoration of Sir George Mackenzie of Roseheugh (1636–1691) founder of the Advocates Library.

Borthwick's Close (186)

Dates from 1450 and in those far off days housed the mansion and gardens as their town house of the Lords Borthwick whose castle was near Middleton, Midlothian. Lord Napier of Merchiston also lived here.

Old Fishmarket Close (190)

(it was also a poultry market). It had at one time been described as 'a steep, narrow stinking ravine.' 'Fish were generally thrown out in the street at the top of the close, dragged down by dirty boys or women and sold unwashed from old, rickety, scaly, wooden tables exposed to rain, dust and filth!'

The City Hangman or 'doomster' dwelt here—the last hangman, John High, died in 1817. The hangman was also called 'the lad in the piot (magpie) coat'—his livery of black or dark grey was ornamented with silver lace.

George Heriot, benefactor and founder of Heriot's Hospital and School, lived here in 1586 and Daniel Defoe is supposed to have worked here as a secret agent for the English Government at the Treaty of Union in 1707. The Union Bank had premises here.

For many years at the head of the close was the Head-quarters of the Fire Brigade's primitive engine. On 'fire!'

being shouted, ropes were seized and the old engine dragged out.

The close was also known as Swift's (in 1709), Fishmarket, Suittie's, Carmichael's and Gourlay's Close.

(St Giles' Cathedral and George IV Bridge/Bank Street lie here).

Mercat Cross; St Giles Cathedral; Parliament House & Parliament Square—see pages 88/89.

Lawnmarket

Brodie's Close (304)

Previously Little's Close, built in 1570—Lord Cullen's, i.e., Sir Francis Grant—Cullin's and South End Entry to Old Bank Closes).

This close took its name from Francis Brodie, Wright (Scots name for a cabinet-maker), glass-grinder and burgess of the City, father and partner of William Brodie of the firm 'Brodie & Son, Wrights & Undertakers, Lawnmarket'.

WILLIAM BRODIE was born in 1741. In manhood he was by day a pious, wealthy and much respected citizen, a regular juryman, burgess and guildbrother of Edinburgh, who, in 1781, was elected Deacon of the Incorporation of Wrights and Town Councillor of the city. But by night he was Edinburgh's most famous criminal hypocrite—a gambler and thief, dissipated and licentious. The annals record that his cunning and audacity were unsurpassed. Robert Louis Stevenson modelled the character of Dr Jekyll and Mr Hyde on this man. He had two mistresses, both of whom bore him a family, and he had a lust for gambling. He therefore needed money.

His plan was a simple one and his story is one of intrigue:

It was customary in the 1780s for Edinburgh shopkeepers to hang their keys upon a nail at the back of their doors, or at least to take no pains to conceal them during the day. Brodie, while working on the premises or calling in for a chat would take impressions of the keys in putty or clay, a piece of which he used to carry in the palm of his hand. He kept a blacksmith, George Smith, another felon, in his pay who forged exact copies of the keys he wanted and with these it was his custom to open the shops of his fellow-tradesmen during the night and remove whatever he fancied.

Some of the goods stolen by him were listed as:

The silver mace of the University of Edinburgh; Silks and other fabrics valued at £400 from Inglis & Horner by the Mercat Cross; 350 pounds of fine black tea from Carnegie the Grocers in Leith, and 10 watches and other jewellery from Bruce's in the North Bridge valued at £300.

Later two other villains were added to his gang (Andrew Ainslie and John Brown). They carried out many robberies together. Then came the big one —the General Excise Office— to allow Brodie to retire in comfort. At that time the General Excise Office for Scotland was housed in a mansionhouse in Chessel's Court, containing the revenues and collected taxes of the King's Scottish subjects. After carrying out his normal ritual with the putty Brodie and the gang gained access on a dark winter night and ransacked the place, failing to gain much except for a mere £16. The gang accused Brodie for the failure of the exercise. John Brown in order to secure a reward gave evidence of a previous robbery but did not mention Brodie by name. Brodie fearful of his own life fled the country. Brown then confessed everything and a reward of £200 was put on Brodie's head. He was described as a sallow faced man with a queer way of walking and a scar under one eye.

The following advertisement was issued at the time by the Sheriff Clerk's office:

Two hundred pounds reward—Whereas William Brodie, a considerable House-Carpenter and Burgess of the City of Edinburgh, has been charged with being concerned in breaking into the General Excise Office for Scotland and stealing from the Cashier's office there a sum of money—and as the said William Brodie has either made his escape from Edinburgh, or is still concealed about that place—a reward of one hundred and fifty pounds sterling is hereby offered to any person who will produce him alive at the Sheriff Clerk's Office, Edinburgh or will secure him, so as he may be brought there within a month from this date; and fifty pounds sterling more, payable upon his conviction, by William Scott, Procurator Fiscal for the Shire of Edinburgh.

He was pursued to Holland and arrested at Amsterdam. Extradited to Edinburgh, his trial took place on 27 August 1788. At it he appeared in full dress, black clothes, silk and his deportment was composed and gentlemanlike.

Pronounced guilty he was sentenced to death on 1 October. Legend has it that he was the first criminal to die on a new gallows ironically designed by himself. In truth he was executed on the gibbet, after making a great show of inspecting the apparatus, along with his accomplice, George Smith, on top of a single storey building extended from the Old Tolbooth and before a countless multitude. It took three attempts to hang him before the hangman achieved success. Gossip had it that Brodie had bribed the hangman to adjust the rope in order to avoid dislocation of his neck; others said that he had been given a small metal tube to insert in his throat to prevent suffocation and his body had been wired down both sides to soften the jerk of the drop. In any case all these efforts failed and he was pronounced dead. He is buried at the north-east corner of the now disused Buccleuch Parish Church burial ground in Chapel Street. The grave is unmarked.

Brodie's Close originally extended from the Lawnmarket down to the Cowgate until Victoria Street was built. The house of the Brodie family no longer exists, since it was demolished in 1835. On the opposite side of the street is Deacon Brodie's Tavern, named after the infamous Deacon; a mural on the side wall describes the villain.

DEACON BRODIE

BORN 28TH Sept. 1741
EXECUTED 1st Oct. 1788

William Brodie, Deacon of Wrights & Masons of Edinburgh was the son of a cabinet maker in the Lawnmarket He was born in Brodies Close and hanged near St Giles – both places being just a few steps from the tavern which now bears his name.

In manhood, Brodies baseness inspired Robert Louis Stevenson to write that famous classic – Dr Jekyll and Mr Hyde By day, William Brodie was pious, wealthy and a much respected citizen and in 1781 was elected Deacon Councillor of the city. But at night, he was a gambler, a thief, dissipated and licentious, The annals record: 'His cunning and audacity were unsurpassed'

Brodie was hanged from the citys new gallows on Oct 1st 1788. Ironically, he himself had designed the gallows that were eventually to seal his fate.

Signcraft 031-228 2220

Mural on the side of 'Deacon Brodie's Tavern' Lawnmarket. (Deacon Brodie's bars are now in existence in Chicago, South Dakota, and Michigan, and are always packed out with people curious about Brodie and Scotland).

Fisher's Close (312)

(Previously known as Hamilton's Close and Cant's Land).

Leads down to Victoria Terrace. A house owned by the Duke of Buccleuch's family had to be demolished in 1835 to allow for the construction of Victoria Street. Prior to this it led steeply down to the Cowgate.

Named after Thomas Fisher, merchant, who built and resided in a tenement here; in 1595 he was sent by the Convention of Royal Burghs on a special mission to the French Court. He was the first Chamberlain of the City.

In recent years the close contained the administration offices of the National Library of Scotland.

Riddle's Close & Court (322)

Formerly Sir John Smith's Close. (He was Lord Provost in 1643) Royston's Close, Shaw's Close, and McMorran's Close.

Takes its name from 'Riddal's Land', dating from 1587 and built by George Riddell, wright and burgess. Being an enclosed court it was intended to be capable of defence. The court is bounded by L-shaped three-storey houses. The interiors have fine beam and plaster ceilings and wood panelling, and the houses are fine examples of the style in which merchants lived in the 18th century. There is a turret staircase outside the building.

David Hume lived in the close for a short while before settling in James' Court.

A rich merchant and Bailie, John McMorran, lived and carried on business here. He was City Treasurer from 1589 to 1591. His house was on the first floor, reached by a stone stair near the corner of the court—like stepping back into the 16th century.

In 1595 the youths of the High School (built in 1578 in the grounds of the Blackfriars' Monastery) were not pleased about a reduction in their holidays and barricaded themselves in the school, with some food, threatening not to surrender until the magistrates had given in to their demands. The Rector, Hercules Rollock, who had tried to quell the rebellion, called on Bailie McMorran for help. He arrived with a

Inside Riddle's Court in the Lawnmarket.

posse of City officers to deal with them, and ordered the door to be prised open. The boys warned they would shoot him if he tried to break down the door. He took this as an idle threat and carried on. A shot rang out and he fell, shot through the brain. The boys escaped the vengeance of the crowd. The ringleader was William Sinclair, son of the Chancellor of Caithness. He and seven others were taken to the Tolbooth Gaol. The boy escaped the justice called for by virtue of his aristocratic connections; King James VI was consulted; apparently there was no trial, and since the boys were all under 14 they were acquitted 'by His Majesty's express Warrant'.

The acquitted boy lived to be Sir William Sinclair of Mey, ancestor to the titles of the Earl of Caithness.

In 1598 James VI and his Queen Anne of Denmark and her brother, the Duke of Holstein, were banqueted here 'with great solemnity and merriness'.

Other owners and residents were Sir John Smith of Grothall (Provost 1643–46, and father of Lady Gray) and Sir James Mackenzie of Royston.

The Court served the first few years of the Edinburgh Festival as a theatre for the Oxford and Cambridge Players. It has now been restored by Lothian Regional Council as a community Education service. A set of historic 18th-century painted panels were unearthed here in the 1960s during renovation work. They are decorated with landscape scenes by the artist, James Norie, and will form one of the centre-piece displays at the new museum of Scotland depicting Scottish life and culture over the centuries.

Castlehill

Highland Church of Tolbooth St. John's——see Page 90.

Boswell's Court (352)

Although James Boswell (1740–95) is reputed to have dined and presumably lived here with the philosopher and critic Dr Samuel Johnson (1709–84), (also being his biographer) in 1770, the close is actually named after the chief resident, a physician, Dr John Boswell, uncle of James Boswell.

The close was previously known as Lothian's Close from Louthian's Land, owned by Thomas Lothian, Merchant. In the 17th century the Duke of Gordon had a mansion here.

Entrance to Boswell's Court, Castlehill, now 'The Witchery' Restaurant.

The Duchess of Gordon's doorway was built into the 20th-century wall of the former Castlehill School (now the Scotch Whisky Heritage Centre). It is now enclosed within the Witchery Restaurant and can only be seen from inside.

Blair's Close

This is an un-named close adjacent to Cannonball House, built in 1630. Access can be gained from the former school.

This tenement was the one nearest the Castle, owned by Archibald Blair in 1753.

Prior to this the close was called Baird's Close when it was owned by William Baird, merchant, whose father was Sir Robert Baird of Saughtonhall.

The gable of the adjacent Cannonball House contains a cannonball allegedly fired from a cannon in the Castle at Prince Charles Edward Stuart as he approached in 1745. However, an alternative explanation for its existence was to mark the gravitation height of Edinburgh's first piped water-supply in 1681.

PART THREE
Other Points of Interest in the Royal Mile

OUTLOOK TOWER The 'Camera Obscura' just beyond Ramsay Lane in Castlehill presents fascinating views of Edinburgh. The lower parts of the building date from the 17th century, the upper parts being added and opened to the public in 1853. It was then known as Short's Observatory, after an optician, Maria Theresa Short, who devised and built the Camera Obscura. Sir Patrick Geddes owned the building in 1892 and gave it its present name when he developed it as a sociological museum. From the top of the tower high above the city, extraordinary views open up in all directions to the visitor through the expert deployment of revolving lenses and mirrors.

GLADSTONE'S LAND, Lawnmarket. Until the National Trust for Scotland took it over in 1934 Gladstone's Land was a slum, but it was restored in 1935 by Sir Frank Mears. It is now a museum to the life of the street itself, having been re-equipped with contemporary furnishings. Built about 1550 and extended in 1617–20, this six-storey narrow tenement was acquired by a merchant and burgess, Thomas Gledstanes, who gave it its name. Open to the public, it has, like many houses of its time, unusual original painted ceilings, wall paintings, and original fireplaces.

THE CITY CHAMBERS in the High Street opposite St Giles. To a design of John Adam in 1753 Lord Provost George Drummond ordered the construction of a beautiful building in a discreet square, to be used as a Royal Exchange—a place where merchants, lawyers, and others engaged in commerce could meet for business. It was erected in 1761 on the site of a house built by Sir Simon Preston of Craigmillar, where Mary Queen of Scots spent her last night of freedom before her imprisonment in Leven Castle. However, the purpose of Drummond's dream failed, and the building eventually fell to the Town Council in 1811, then to Edinburgh Corporation (later Edinburgh District Council) and was renamed 'the City Chambers'. The rear elevation of twelve storeys is one of the tallest buildings remaining in the Old Town. Mary King's and Allan's closes lie below the buildings of the City Chambers.

MOUBRAY HOUSE in the High Street (next to John Knox House) is a 16th–17th-century development having 15th-century origins dating from about 1451. Said to be one of the oldest in the city it was a tavern in the 18th century. In 1890 the upper floors were a temperance hotel. Here Daniel Defoe lived when he edited the *Edinburgh Courant* in 1710; he was the author of *Robinson Crusoe* and was also suspected of being an English government agent when the Treaty of Union with England was approved in 1707; he was supposedly pelted with stones and rubbish when he looked out of his window in Moubray House. There is a plaque on the wall here to an artist, George Jamesone (1588–1644).

JOHN KNOX HOUSE in the High Street dates from about 1490, being the last timber-galleried house and one of the oldest in Edinburgh. Originally in 1556 it belonged to Mariota Arres and her husband, James Mossman, goldsmith to Mary, Queen of Scots. Their initials decorate the outside. It was supposedly the home of the Reformer for a short spell between the years 1561 and 1572. This is subject to doubt, since there is little evidence that he ever lived there, although tradition has kept the legend alive. By 1849 the house was in a ruinous state, but it was repaired and brought up to standard when plans for widening the street were proposed. The Church of Scotland bought the property in 1853 and it became a museum, being further restored over 100 years later.

NETHERBOW PORT. The Netherbow Arts centre is named

Moubray House and John Knox House two of the oldest in Edinburgh.

after Netherbow Port (built in 1513) or lower gate of Edinburgh—one of the six curfewed gateways to Edinburgh this one dividing the two burghs of Edinburgh and the Canongate. The site of the gate is marked by brass cobbles in the road at the point in the Royal Mile where the High Street becomes the Canongate at Jeffrey Street/St Mary's Street. Cobbles also mark the position of the Flodden Wall. The 17th century bell within the main door of the Centre is from the original gate. Cast in Holland it was removed from the gatehouse when it was demolished in 1764. A model of the Port hangs

Netherbow Arts Centre with a model of the old Netherbow Port.

on the wall outside. The heads of criminals and preachers were originally displayed on the Port. The sculptured stone panel on view in Netherbow Courtyard was also removed from the gatehouse. Dated 1606 it commemorates the marriage of James VI to Anne of Denmark. The cipher of the Scottish Crown which it contains has been cut out and then restored in different stone possibly as a result of Cromwell's occupation of Scotland. The Art Centre is owned by the

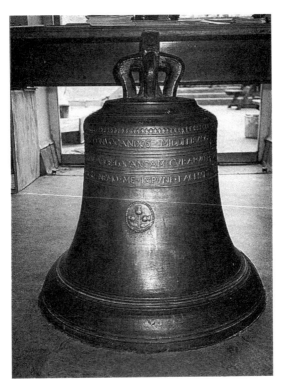

The 17th century bell from the old Netherbow Port within the entrance to the Netherbow Arts Centre.

Church of Scotland. Built on the site of the former Moray-Knox Church it is a sign of the close relationship between Church and Nation which is part of Scotland's heritage.

CANONGATE TOLBOOTH, 163 Canongate. At one time the Canongate was a separate burgh outside Edinburgh's walls, the Tolbooth being one of the gateways into Edinburgh and a Civic Centre in 1592. Between 1842 and 1848 it served as an overflow for Calton Jail before it underwent restoration in 1879. The clock itself dates from 1879. An impressive three-storey building with an adjoining tower, complete with gun loops, it was formerly a council chamber, court-house, and collection place for the independent burgh's dues. It is now a museum telling 'The People's Story', details of which are contained under the entry for Old Tolbooth Wynd on Page 39.

CANONGATE CHURCH. This 17th-century church was built in 1688 by the Catholic James VI of Scotland and II of England from money from the will of Thomas Moodie, to cater for the needs of the congregation from the Abbey Church of Holyrood, when he turned the latter into a Chapel Royal for use of the Knights of the Thistle. It was described by James Grant in *Old and New Edinburgh* as 'a most unpicturesque looking edifice of nameless style with a species of Doric porch.' Here the Queen worships when in residence in Holyrood Palace. Interred in the adjoining kirkyard are several celebrated notaries, among them George Drummond, six times Lord Provost of Edinburgh between 1725 and 1760; Adam Smith, author of *The Wealth of Nations*; Dugald Stewart, philosopher; Robert Hurd, architect (1905–1963), who gained much recognition for his vision and work in the restoration of new buildings in the Canongate; Mrs Agnes McLehose—Burns's 'Clarinda', and Professor James Gregory—inventor of 'Gregory's Mixture', a purgative. The original Mercat Cross of the Canongate can also be seen in the kirkyard.

In recognition of a young fellow poet, Robert Fergusson (1751–1774), whose body was transferred from a pauper's grave to a true and finer resting place here, Robert Burns paid for the erection of a headstone in 1789 over the then unmarked grave with the inscription:

No sculptured marble here nor pompous clay
No storied urn nor animated bust
This simple stone directs pale Scotia's way
To pour her sorrows o'er the Poet's dust.

The detailed account and receipt for the headstone amounting to £5.10s. (£5.50p) can be viewed in the Writers' Museum within Lady Stair's Close.

Born in Edinburgh, Fergusson attended the Royal High School and St Andrews University. Chambers Biographical Dictionary records how 'his company was much sought and convivial excesses permanently injured his health'. He went mad after a head injury, which led to his premature death. Formed in 1994 the 'Robert Fergusson Society' rates Fergusson as Edinburgh's greatest 18th-century poet.

After Prince Charlie's victory at Prestonpans English soldiers taken prisoner were held here. The neighbouring Church manse in Reid's Court was originally built in 1690 as a coaching house and converted for use as a manse in 1789, which it remained until 1832. Thereafter it fell into disrepair until 1958 when it was restored as a manse once more.

—Crossing to the South side of the street we commence the ascent of the Royal Mile—

QUEENSBERRY HOUSE was built in the Canongate in 1681 for Lord Hatton but bought later by William 1st Duke of Queensberry. His son James was the principal promoter of the Treaty of Union of 1707 between Scotland and England which caused great displeasure to the Scottish nation. His insane eldest son, Lord Drumlanrig, was caught here roasting and eating the flesh of a young kitchen lad. The house was at one time a barracks but has long since been used as an old peoples' hospital.

ACHESON HOUSE situated next to Huntly House but offset from the street in the Canongate dates back to 1633 and was built for Sir Archibald Acheson, Secretary of State for Scotland to Charles I. It was restored in 1937 and was formerly the Headquarters of the Scottish Craft Centre.

By pausing here the visitor will see the old original doorway taken from Anchor Close at 241 High Street in 1932 and rebuilt here in 1937.

HUNTLY HOUSE, 149 Canongate, dates from 1570 and was once the home of the Dowager Countess of Gordon, who only stayed in a flat within it. It was purchased by the City in 1924 and is a principal museum of local history packed with collections exhibiting silver, furniture, jewellery, glassware, pottery, and many trade signs, and containing relics of old Edinburgh houses. It also has a copy of the National Covenant signed in Greyfriar's Churchyard in 1638 by citizens as a protest against Charles I's attempt to establish Episcopacy in Scotland and a new Church service. In the 18th century it was the Headquarters of the Canongate smiths (the Hammermen). At one time it was known as the 'speaking house' because of inscriptions mentioned and detailed under the information contained on Page 50 within the heading Bakehouse Close.

MORAY HOUSE has an entry from the Canongate opposite Bible Land. It was built about 1628 for Mary, Dowager Countess of Home, and handed on to her daughter, the Countess of Moray, who gave it its current name. In 1648 Oliver Cromwell made it his Headquarters. It had a royal visitor in the shape of Charles I, and the Treaty of Union between Scotland and England was signed in its garden pavilion in 1707 by the 'parcel of rogues'. For many years it has been a teachers' training college.

THE MUSEUM OF CHILDHOOD is in the High Street, opposite John Knox House. This museum has gained international recognition as being the first in the world devoted solely to childhood history, but it also has a fascination for visitors of all ages. It contains the world's finest collection of games, toys, dolls, hobby items and all sorts of childhood memorabilia handed down through the ages.

Tron Kirk in the High Street.

TRON KIRK in the High Street at the junction with the North and South Bridge. Work on Christ's Church at the Tron began in 1637 and was named after the old public salt-weighing beam or 'tron'. It opened for worship in 1641 intended for an overflow from St Giles. Edinburgh's own 'Great fire' consumed the steeple in 1824. The spire was replaced in 1828 and the church continued as a place of worship until 1952. In 1987 the Edinburgh Old Town Trust stopped the rot in the Kirk. It had been closed for 35 years. In the 1970's excavations found that the medieval alley of Marlin's Wynd had been buried in the Tron's foundations. Here Edinburgh traditionally celebrated the New Year (or 'Hogmanay'—Old Year's Night) before the recent modern celebrations were introduced.

In the summer of 1994 the atmospheric building with its archaeological excavations showing the shape of ancient buildings attracted 130,000 visitors to its temporary visitor 'orientation' centre. Future plans for the building are that it will become a permanent visitor centre.

The Mercat Cross in the east wing of Parliament Square.

THE MERCAT CROSS in the High Street next to St Giles was the point in the Old Town from which Royal Proclamations were, and still are, made. The original dates from 1365. The cross is 19th century but a small part of the shaft comes from the original whereas the base, being a replica, dates from 1885 and was paid for by W.E. Gladstone (a former Prime Minister). The original cross was the scene at which many famous Scots were executed and its site is marked on the roadway nearby. Here it was that the Marquis of Montrose was hanged in 1650.

ST. GILES' CATHEDRAL A church has existed on this site since AD 854, the four central pillars dating from about 1120. It was burned down by the English in 1385 but the building in its present form dates from 1829, although its famous crown steeple dates from 1495 and was repaired by John Mylne in 1648. The Reformers gave the Catholics a rough passage, mass being sung here for the last time in 1560. The year before, John Knox (1514–1572) as appointed minister, had preached his first sermon here. After the Reformation it was divided into four churches and in 1633 briefly became an Episcopal 'Cathedral' for a short period until 1638. Its proper name however is *High Kirk of St Giles*. (The name 'St Giles' is derived from a Greek hermit who settled in Provence in the 6th century and was the patron saint of beggars and criminals). There was a famous incident here in 1637 when a town resident, Jenny Geddes, a vegetable seller, threw a stool at the preacher, the Bishop of Edinburgh, who attempted to read a newly-introduced English Liturgy and dared 'sing masse in ma lugge' [ear]. At one time, in 1643, one of the vaults was used to store gunpowder, and parts of the building were used as a police office and prison. The unique Thistle Chapel is open to the public. St Giles' is known as the Mother Church of World Presbyterianism. Near the Cathedral in the 17/18th

Religious Reformer John Knox within St Giles' Cathedral.

centuries little shops called 'Luckenbooths' (or 'Locked Booths') were traditionally the centre of the jewellery trade. From about 1700 Luckenbooth brooches were given as love tokens or charms.

The building of *PARLIAMENT HOUSE* (now Parliament Hall) in 1632 in Parliament Square on the far side of St Giles was intended to replace The Castle or the Tolbooth as the

Parliament of Scotland by a proposal from Charles I. It served this purpose from 1639 to 1707, when Westminster took over this service at the Union of the Scottish and English Parliaments. The Supreme Law Court of Scotland took over after the politicians left, and the building now houses the High Court, Court of Session and the Signet Library. The High Court—where some of Scotland's biggest criminal trials have been held—has been housed here but is due for relocation in the mid to late 1990s in the city's former Sheriff Court across the Royal Mile. However civil cases and appeals will remain at Parliament House. Nowadays advocates and writers meet to discuss cases with the unusual practice of walking to and fro dressed in their wigs and robes. The Hall is lined with some handsome paintings and contains a beautiful 17th-century hammer-beam roof and stained-glass windows representing the inauguration in 1532 of the Court of Session by James V. Below is the Laigh [low] Hall which was once used by Oliver Cromwell as a stable.

PARLIAMENT SQUARE (or 'Close' as it once was) surrounds St Giles to the West, South and East. It has to the east, behind St Giles, a statue of Charles II mounted on horseback and placed strategically over the remains of John Knox in what was previously St Giles' kirkyard. It is the oldest equestrian statue in Britain, erected in 1688. The burial ground built over during the construction of Parliament House was the main one of the Old Town until 1532. Within St Giles itself is a statue to the religious reformer, John Knox, erected in 1906 and overlooking his grave. This vicinity was at one time 'the busiest and most populous nook of the Old Town'. Another statue in the Square, unveiled in 1888, is a memorial to Walter Francis Montague Douglas Scott, 5th Duke of Buccleuch and 7th Duke of Queensberry KG—it is known as The Buccleuch Statue. Around the close (i.e. Parliament Close) which stood near here a major fire in 1700 destroyed many buildings—some 14 storeys high—making 400 families homeless.

The site of the *OLD EDINBURGH TOLBOOTH* in front of St Giles is marked by a heart-shaped pattern of granite setts embedded in the road. The outline of the building is also marked on the road with brass plates. The Old Tolbooth was demolished in 1817, having served Edinburgh for over 400 years as a Council Chamber, a courthouse, a toll-collection point, a prison, and a place of execution. At various times in the past it accommodated the Scottish Parliament, Edinburgh Town Council, and the Courts of Law. As a jail it was immortalised by Sir Walter Scott in *The Heart of Midlothian*. Peculiarly it is an old Edinburgh custom to spit on the centre spot of the heart for luck.

THE HIGHLAND CHURCH OF TOLBOOTH ST JOHN'S at the junction of Castlehill, Johnston Terrace, and the Lawnmarket was designed by James Gillespie Graham and Augustus W.N. Pugin, and was completed in 1844 for the General Assembly of the Church of Scotland. It has the highest spire in the city, being 240 feet high. Until it was taken over in 1984 for use as a Heritage Centre services on Sunday afternoons were held in Gaelic.

CANNONBALL HOUSE in Castlehill has a religious motto: 'O Lord in Thee is al mi Traist' over the lintel. Built in 1630 by a furrier called Mure, it is said to have received its name from a ball lodged in the west wall having been fired at the Jacobite siege in 1745. An alternative explanation for its existence was to mark the gravitation height of Edinburgh's first piped water supply in 1681.

PART FOUR
'The Nor' Loch'

Since many of the steep and narrow Castlehill, Lawnmarket, and High Street closes of old descended to the now long since gone Nor' (or North) Loch, it would seem appropriate to include the historical background to this man-made feature.

First of all let us briefly witness the scene:

'Let her droon!'

'Wha's next fur dookin'? [ducking]

Excitement rose to fever pitch amongst the crowd of idlers gathered on the loch-shore around a crude see-saw construction. Strapped to a rough seat at one end of it was a haggard, crudely dressed woman in her late fifties. Convicted of witchcraft or some other crime she was being publicly punished for her sins by 'ducking' to the obvious delight and amusement of the local inhabitants. Nearby, under the hot sun, all kinds of refuse and impurities lay strewn about. Water rats and eels darted to and fro. The stench was putrid . . .

Hard to believe though it may seem, this scene occurred in Edinburgh's Princes Street Gardens over three centuries ago.

'But where is the loch in Princes Street Gardens?' the visitor may ask.

Today the North or Nor' Loch has either never been heard of or is a hazily mentioned memento from the mystic past. In by days gone by however, it was a reality stretching from St Cuthbert's Church at the West end of what is now Princes Street, through the valley hollowed out by glacial action in the Ice Age which divided the Old Town from the New Town, to Netherbow Port and the site of Waverley Station in the East.

But where did it come from, what purpose did it serve and what happened to it?

In the 15th century King James II feeling less secure than his predecessors hit upon the idea of protecting the North

A view of Edinburgh Castle taken from the top of the Scott Monument showing the Mound and the original site of the old Nor' Loch with St. Cuthbert's Church in the distance.

side of the town from the old enemies from over the Border between Scotland and England by forming a water barrier along one side of the old Edinburgh Castle. The original intention was to make a moat with the waters from a spring situated at the base of Castle Rock, but when it was discovered that the water there was so plentiful it was decided to form a permanent loch controlled by a dam and a sluice with the added security of a wall containing the Wellhouse Tower. Thus it remained a protective barrier for three centuries, keeping would-be aggressors from attacking the north side of the castle.

At first the new loch was recognised as a feature of great beauty over-shadowed by the majestic castle. Terraced gardens are believed to have sloped down to it from the original Old Town quarters of the Lawnmarket, Castlehill, and the High Street, and it was dotted here and there with pleasure boats and swans. All too soon, however, it became a dumping ground for all kinds of rubbish and was consequently rat-infested. In 1655 it was even recorded that some thousands of eels were cast upon its banks after some stormy weather.

During its early existence ducking and even drowning in the Nor' Loch were frequent forms of punishment, inflicted mainly upon females. It became the haunt of all sorts of idle people and a place of amusement for the citizens.

While draining operations were taking place early in the 19th century workmen discovered a large coffin of thick fir deals containing one male and two female skeletons. They were believed to have been the remains of a man called Sinclair, and his two sisters, with both of whom he was convicted of having committed incest in 1628, when sentence of drowning was administered.

Drowning was not always administered, however. Overall the average depth of the water reached to about eight feet, but in some parts it plumbed a depth of fifteen feet. Such pools were great attractions for suicides. Instances of ducking occurred up to 1660, but thereafter they became rare, and ceased altogether by 1685. Between the mid-16th and mid-18th centuries, however, it was estimated that about 150 persons had been drowned in the Nor' Loch, the majority of which were suicides.

It eventually became clear that the loch was not being maintained for the purpose of defence or amenity but was in fact a means of keeping smuggling low. For a period, smugglers were afforded ready facilities for getting wines and forbidden items into the city gates free of import and customs duties, the loch being conveniently situated at the foot of the Old Town closes or entries. However, this was soon brought under control.

By 1753 soil from the town was constantly running into the loch and it was almost half filled in. The building of the

North Bridge in 1763, connecting the Old Town with the New, reduced the size of the loch, mainly because the bridge had to be built on dry land.

An Old Town 18th-century clothier, GEORGE BOYD was the first to recognise the need for an easy crossing to see for himself the new buildings springing up on the North side of the loch. The muddy quagmire presented the problem however. Being anxious to provide access for his New Town customers to his Old Town shop he and some neighbours laid stepping stones over the marsh.

His project was officially taken up by the City authorities and between 1781 and 1830 another construction linking the Old with the New contracted the loch even further by dividing the bed into two parts, thus stopping the flow of water from West to East. This was the Mound described by James Grant in his *Old and New Edinburgh* as an 'elongated hill, like a huge railway embankment, a clumsy, enormous and unremovable substitute for a bridge'.

The Lord Provost at the time gained permission to dump rubbish from the new streets being constructed in the New Town on to the 'earthen mound' so that 'between 1781 and 1830' Grant recorded 'augmentations to its breadth and height were continually made, till it became the mighty mass it is.' But the foresight of 'Geordie Boyd's Mud Brig' remained a vital link between the Old & New. When completed it was estimated that the Mound contained over two million cartloads of rubbish.

Life in the Old Town was coming to an end at the turn of the 19th century when the rich abandoned it to the poor. Crowds would gather to watch 'The Great Flitting' as paintings, crockery and fine furniture were piled on to carts for the bumpy journey down The Mound to the New Town.

As the much-reduced remains of the original loch were, by 1787, serving no useful purpose and were becoming stagnant the Town Council ordered it to be drained with all possible speed. Thirty years later the portion west of the Mound which now houses the Ross Bandstand, centre of open-air summer entertainment, was described as an 'impassible fetid marsh'. By 1821 it had been converted into a pleasure ground, but the portion east of the Mound remained a reedy marshy hollow long after the loch had disappeared.

While sitting in Princes Street Gardens today, either gazing up at the bold outline of the Castle perched high upon its rock, admiring the beauty and layout of the famous floral clock, enjoying the peaceful setting of the Royal Scots Memorial crescent of garden, or merely watching the trains go by or photographing the waters bursting over the Ross Fountain, it is difficult to imagine that this area was once a man-made loch, scene of many tragedies, and yet, looking upon it through half-closed eyelids the sounds of water splashing round one end of a see-saw accompanied by the screams of some poor unfortunate 'witch' or lapping the bows of a smuggler's craft on a dark misty night do not seem so far off and conjure up a beauty of a different sort.

Although not realised the source of the old Nor' Loch is still 'active' today! It is located at the base of the Castle Rock, on the South side of the railway line skirting Princes Street Gardens and marked by the following inscription:

'St. Margaret's Well'

The fountain of the Ancient Wellhouse Tower celebrated in the history of the Castle since the time of St. Margaret, Queen of Scotland in the 11th century.

It was restored by the officers of the 93rd Sutherland Highlanders in 1873.

Visitors to the much admired Gardens need have no fear of the Nor' Loch re-appearing and bursting its banks, however, since water from the original spring is now controlled

St. Margaret's Well, Princes Street gardens.

and diverted by sewer through the Gardens to beyond Holyrood Palace about two miles away!

They may also wish to know that although some witches were ducked or drowned in the Nor' Loch others were burned at the stake at a site near the Castle. A disused fountain at the north side of the entrance to the Castle Esplanade carries the following inscription:

> This fountain designed by John Duncan is near the site on which many witches were burned at the stake. The wicked head and serene head signify that some used their exceptional knowledge

for evil purposes while others were misunderstood and wished their kind nothing but good.

The serpent was the dual significance of evil and wisdom. The foxglove spray further emphasises the dual purpose of many common objects.

There follows a list of the names of 497 closes, wynds, entries, or courts, either no longer in existence or renamed many times. Most are self-explanatory, but the origin or history of the more unusual and interesting ones is given at the end. The current name is shown against the old name if known, and all are closes unless otherwise stated.

OBSOLETE NAME..... CURRENT NAME

Abbey
Abbot of Melrose's
Abernethy's ....Allan's
Adamson's
Aikman's ....Dickson's
Aitken's
Alexander Cant's..Cant's
Alexr
  Dennistoun's.....Craig's
Alexr. Don's
Alexander King's..Mary King's
Alexander
  Lindsay's ....Bishop's
Alexr. Uddart's
Alexander
  Young's ....Tweeddale Court
Alison's
Alley
Anchor Tavern
  in Fuller's
  Close...............Anchor
Archibald's
Assembly............Old Assembly
Ayr Bank
Back of Bell's
  Wynd...............New Assembly
Back of Best
  Wynd
Back of
  Borthwick's

Bailie Clark's
Bailie Gentle's
Bailie Grant's
Bailie Nairn's
Bailie Reid's ...... Reid's
Bailie Sandilands'
Baird's .... Blair's
Baker's .... Brodie's
Ballantyne's
Bannager's
Barclay's
Barne's............. Old Assembly
Baron Grant's
Barrie's .... Bailie Fyfe's
Barringer's
Barron's............ Old Post Office
Barry's .... Bailie Fyfe's
Bass Wynd
Bassendean's ...... Fountain
Bassendyne's ...... Baron Maule's
Bath's Wynd
Baxter's
Beith's Wynd
Bell's
Bess Wynd
Best's Wynd
Bestis Wynd
Beth's Wynd
Big Jack's
Big Lochend.
Birnie's............. Craig's

Bishop's Land. ....Bishop's
Bishop of
  Murray's.
Blackfriar's Wynd.
Blacklock's.
Blyth's. ....Reid's Court
Bowling Green. ...Gladstone Court
Boyd's. ....Chalmer's
Broun's.
Brown's Court.
Brownhill's
  Court. ....James Court
Bruce's. ....Warriston's
Bryson's. ....Trunk's
Buchanan's Court
Cachepool.
Caichpeele
Caithness
Callender's.........Morrison's
Cambrone's
Cameron's
Cantore's
Cap & Feather
Carfrae's
Carmichael's.......Craig's.
Carrutherber's.....Carrubber's
Carruther's
Carthrae's
Catchkan's
Cathkin's
Celler's
Chamber's..........Chalmer's
Chancellor's
Charteris ....Hyndford's
Cheyne's
Clark's
Coalstoun's
Cockburn's.........Bailie Fyfe's
Coitken's
Collington's ....Hyndford's

Collingtoun's
Colston's
Commercial
  Bank .... New Assembly
Common .... Mid Common
Common
  Bakehouse
Con's
Conn's
Cooper's
Cordiner's .... Bakehouse
Coudon's
Coulis
Coull's
Coult's
Council Chamber
Coutt's
Coyne-house....... South Gray's
Coynie.............. South Gray's
Crammy's
Cranston's .... Mylne's court
Crichton's
Crook's
Cruick's
Cullen's .... Brodie's
Cullin
Cumming's
Currey's
Currie's
Currouris
Dallas.............. Old Playhouse
Dark Shoemaker's
David
  Stevenson's....... Fountain
Davidson's......... White Horse
Deasyre's .... Chalmer's
Dempster's
Dennistoun's...... Craig's
Densquer's......... Chalmer's
Dixon's............. Dickson's

Dr. Drummond's..Bull's
Dr. Hope's ....Hope's Court
Dr. Seton's
Dr. Sinclair's
Don's
Donaldson's
Dougal's ....Allan's
Douglas' ....Allan's
Doul's ....Allan's
Dowel's..............Allan's
Drummond's.......Bull's
Duell's..............Allan's
Duncan's
Duncan
  Campbell's
Dunlop's ....Allan's
Dunsyre's ....Chalmer's
Durie's ....Old Assembly
East Bailie
  Fyfe's..............Paisley
East Common
East Fleshmarket
East Jack's
East Lochend's ....Lochend
East Shoemaker's
Eastmost Fyfe's
Edward Hope's
Edward Nisbet's...Bishop's
Elliot's
Elphinson Court
Entry to Bowling
  Grn ....Gladstone Ct
Exchange
Fairden's ....James Court
Fairholm's
Fairlie's Entry
  from Cowgate ....New Assembly
Falcon's
Falconer's
Falcord's
Ferrie's

Finlayson's
Fishmarket......... Old Fishmarket
Fishmercate........ Old Fishmarket
Fleming's .... Monteith's
Foord's
Ford's Row .... Bull's
Fordyce............. Anchor
Forres
Forrester's Wynd
Forstar's
Fortune's........... Old Stamp
                    Office
Foster's
Foular's .... Anchor
Foules
Foulis............... North Foulis
Fountainhall...... James Court
Fowlar's............ Anchor
Fowler's .... North Foulis
Fowlis .... North Foulis
Fuird's
Fuller's............. Anchor
Fullarton's .... Fountain
Galloway's
Gentle's
Gillespie's .... Old Assembly
Gillespy's .... Old Assembly
Gillilan's .... Gullan's
Gillon's .... Gullan's
Gladstane's........ James Court
Gloucester Gate... Forsyth's
Goolan's .... Gullan's
Goolen's .... Gullan's
Gooseford's
Gordon's
Gosford's
Gourlay's .... Old Fishmarket
Grant's
Grant's Little
Gray's.............. North Gray's
Greig's

Haddington's Entry .... Reid's
Hair's
Halbertoune
Haliburton's .... Craig's
Halkerston's Wynd
Halkertoune
Hamilton's .... Fisher's
Hammermen's ..... Bakehouse
Hangman's
Hart's
Hartis
Hastie's
Heart's
Henderson's .... Wardrop's Court
Heriot's
High School
Hodge's
Home's .... Advocate's
Hopper's
Hugh Brown's
Hume's
Humph's .... Old Fishmarket
Hunter's
Huntly .... Bakehouse
Hutcheson's .... Geddes Entry
Inglis .... Old Playhouse
Ireland's
Ironside Court
Jack's
Jacob Barron's ..... Old Post Office
Jairden's .... James' Court
James Bayne's
James Brown's ..... Tweeddale Ct
James Nisbet's ..... Bishop's
Jameson's
Jardine's .... James' Court
John Barton's ...... Fountain
John Baxton's

John Dickson of Hartree ...... James' Court
John Laing's ...... Tweeddale Court
John McMorran's ..... Riddle's
John Morison's .... Morrison's
John Young's
Johnston's .... Burnet's
Josiah's. .... Craig's
Joussie's .... Craig's
Joussy's
Joysie's .... Craig's
Kelloch's
Kennedy's .... Stevenlaw's
Killoch's
Kilkerran's Court
King's .... Mary King's
Kinloch's
Kinnaird's
Kintore's
Kintyre's
Kirkheugh
Knowis
Knox
Lady Gray's .... Lady Stair's
Lady Menzies
Lady Minnies'
Lady St. Ninian's
Lamont's Land .... Bull's
Lauder's .... Byres'
Laurence Ord's .... White Horse
Lee's
Leitche's .... Allan's
Leith's .... Allan's
Leith Wynd
Leithe's .... Allan's
Libberton's Wynd
Lindsay's .... Bishop's
Little's .... Old Post Office
Little Grant's

Little Jack's
Little Shoemaker's
Livingstoun's
Lockhart's Court
Logan's
Lord Colston's
Lord Cullen's ...... Brodie's
Lord Durie's .... Borthwick's
Lord Morton's
Lord Streighan's
Lord Strichen's
Lothian's .... Boswell's Court
Lower Baxter's
McGregor's
McGrigor's
McKell's .... Panmure.
Macmorran's ...... Riddle's Court
Magdalene
  Entry .... Gladstone Court
Malcolme's .... Byres'
Malloch's
Marlin's Wynd
Marquis of
  Lothian's
Marquis of
  Tweeddale's ...... Tweeddale Court
Mauchan's
Mauchine's
Mausey Smith's
Mausie Smith's
May
  Drummond's ..... Bull's
Merlin's Wynd
Mid Baxter's
Middle Baxter's ... Wardrop's Court
Middle
  Common .... Mid Common
Middle Fleshmarket
Mill's
Miller's

Miln's
Mint .... South Gray's
Mitchell's
Moffat's
Monroe's
Morocco's
Moscrop's
Moubray's .... Fountain
Mowbray's
Mrs Minish's
Mrs Muir's
Munloch's
Murdoch's
Murray's .... New Assembly
Nairne's
Nether
  Lochend's .... Lochend
Netherys
New Logan's
Newbank .... Old Stamp
                             Office
Newton's
Niddry's
Nithrie's
Nudreis
Old Bank .... Old Stamp
                             Office
Old Baxter's
Old Door Stile
Old Fleshmarket
Old
  Greenmarket ..... Fleshmarket
Old High School
Old Lyon's .... Lyon's
Old Meal Market
Old Post House ... Old Post Office
Old Provost's
Old Royal Bank
Old Ship .... Old Stamp
                             Office

Oliphant's

Oliver's

Ord's .... White Horse

Orrock's

Parliament

Paterson's .... Brown's

Paterson's Court

Patrick Nisbet's ... Bishop's

Patrick Shiell's .... Old Assembly

Pearson's

Peebles Wynd

Penman's

Penston's

Perrie's

Perry's

Peter's

Pierie's

Pierry's

Pipe's

Pirie's

Plainstanes

Playhouse

Potter's

Power's

Powrie's

Preston's

Provost's .... Fleshmarket

Provost
  Stewart's .... Advocate's

Purves'

Purvis .... Trunk's

Rae's .... Campbell's

Ramsay's

Rea's

Reid's Coach
  Yard .... Reid's Court

Reid's Yard .... Reid's Court

Richardson's .... Geddes Entry

Robert Gibb's ...... Gibb's

Robertson's Court

Rochead's Court

Rockvail's

Rockville's

Ronald's

Rosehaugh's

Ross's

Ross's Court

Roxburgh's

Royal Bank

Royston's .... Riddle's Court

St. Mannans

St. Mary's Wynd

St Monans Wynd

St. Ninian's

Salutation

Sandeman's

Sandilands'

Sclater's

Scot's

Seaton's

Sempill's .... Semple's

Sellar's

Seton's

Shaw's .... Riddle's Court

Sheel's

Shepherd's Court

Ship .... Old Stamp
                      Office

Ship Tavern .... Old Stamp
                      Office

Shoemaker's .... Bible Land

Sir James
  Stewart's .... Advocate's

Sir John
  Smith's .... Riddle's Court

Slater's

Smith's .... Paisley

Snadonis

Snadoun's

Snawdoun's .... New Assembly

Society .... Baron Maule's
Sommerville's...... Brown's
South End Entry
  to Old Bank
  Close............... Brodie's
South Foulis
Stair's .... Lady Stair's
Stalker's............. Lyon's
Stanelaw's .... Stevenlaw's
Stanfield's .... World's End
Steele's
Steil's............... Old Assembly
Stevenson's......... Fountain
Stewart's .... Advocate's
Stiel's............... Old Assembly
Stinking
Stirling's .... Trunk's
Stonelaw's .... Stevenlaw's
Strachan's .... Forsyth's
Strathie's
Straton's
Stricken's........... (now incorporated
                      within the Scandic
                      Hotel)
Stripping
Stuart's
Suittie's .... Old Fishmarket
Swan's
Sweit's.............. World's End
Swift's .... Old Fishmarket
Swyft's
Tailyifiar's .... Stevenlaw's
Tait's
Tanner's
Tavernour's
Telfer's .... Stevenlaw's
Telpher's .... Stevenlaw's
Tennent's
Thomson's
Tod's

Toddis
Toderick's .... Toddrick's
Touring's .... Trunk's
Touris .... Mary King's
Towris.............. Mary King's
Towrs............... Mary King's
Trotter's .... Bailie Fyfe's
Turk's
Tweedale's......... Tweeddale
                     Court
Uddart's
Udwart's
Upper Baxter's
Upper
  Playhouse .... Old Playhouse
Uppermost
  Baxter's
Vallen's .... Vallence's Entry
Vallene's........... Vallence's Entry
Valentine's .... Vallence's Entry
Vietche's .... Mid Common
Walker's
Walter Willie's
Warden's
Wardlaw's
Watson's
Wauchope
Webster's
Weir's
West Common
Whitslade's........ James' Court
Wilkie's
William
  Bothwell's
William Lothian's
Williamson's...... Semple's
Wilson's Court
Year's
Young's .... Tweeddale Court
Zair's .... Old Assembly

The reader will have found the spelling of some of these names most odd, since they have been handed down from generation to generation by word of mouth, e.g., 'Celler's' for Sellars, 'Fishmercate' for Fishmarket, 'Jairden's' for Jardine's, 'Nudreis' for Niddry's, and 'Telpher's' or 'Tailyifiar's' for Telfer's!

Many of the old close names are self-explanatory, being the name of the chief resident or landowner, but the reader might be interested in the tales or the history behind a few of these long since obsolete ones:

Cap & Feather Close. Named after the 'Cap & Feather Tavern', swept away on the construction of the North Bridge; Robert Fergusson, poet, born here in 1750, was hailed at the age of twenty-one as successor to Allan Ramsay; he died in 1774 in 'Bedlam' asylum near Bristo Port after a fall down steps. Robert Burns placed a tombstone over his grave in Canongate Churchyard.

The Close still runs under the foundations of the *Evening News* building and was the subject of ghostly apparitions which shocked staff as recently as 1994.

The old 13 storey building stands in an area described by many experts to be 'buzzing with psychic energies':—

The mysterious silent figure of an old printer wearing matching brown trousers and jersey with a blue apron tied at the back has been seen striding purposefully along a corridor. In his arms he carried a big heavy wooden tray filled with bits of metal the size of match boxes. He had apparently walked through a door which had been locked for at least a month.

Front counter staff have regular encounters with a supernatural being which brushes past them and by visits from a mischievous spirit of a young blonde woman dressed in black. A security guard also came face to face with the ghost of an employee who died in 1990.

Halkerston's Wynd. A very old wynd of the 1500s, leading to the north. It was a very difficult pedestrian short-cut which could only be used in dry weather. The British Linen Co. Ltd. was started here in 1746 as a note-issuing bank, trading first from this wynd. Named after Halkerston, Clerk of Works, killed while defending the town against the English in 1544.

High School Close. Housed the Burgh High School founded by Members of Holyrood referred to in a Charter by James V in 1529.

Leith Wynd. Was at the east end of the Nor' Loch— demolished in 1848 to allow for the building of Waverley Station.

Libberton's Wynd. Was at the junction of what is now the High Street and George IV Bridge, and could at one time be traced back to 1474. The old close is now covered by Lothian Regional Council old buildings and the National Library of Scotland. It was here that the murderer William Burke of Burke & Hare was executed on 28 January 1829.

It was while carrying out my research into these gems of old Edinburgh that I quite by chance came across a worn and much folded note from ROBERT BURNS encased in a locked display cabinet in the Museum of Antiquities, Queen Street, Edinburgh. I quote directly from the poem it contains. The blanks are as detailed in the note and no doubt referred to acquaintances of the writer and the recipient. Although I have searched through the complete works of Robert Burns for this poem I have failed to find any reference to it. There are possibly many more like it, written to friends and acquaintances, but never committed to print within a volume of the poet's work:

> Mr John Dowie, Libberton's Wynd, Edinburgh.
>
> Dear Johnnie,
>
> I cannot with-hold this tribute of my gratitude from you, in whose house I have spent so many agreeable evenings over a bottle of your three-and-a-halfpenny Ale—If this can add any thing to your fame, as an honest publican, or give a higher value to your cheering Ale, I shall be very happy, and think myself fully rewarded for my trouble. I expect that you will not with-hold from your nightly visitants a sight of this your 'ALE' in order to shew them how highly pleased some of your Customers are with it.——May you enjoy all the happiness which can result from a consciousness of having sold nothing but good, tight wholesome Ale, is the wish of, Dear Johnnie, Your Friend and Customer, (Signed) Robert Burns.
>
> (Edinburgh, 14th Sept 1789.)

JOHNNIE DOWIE'S ALE

A' ye wha' wis on e'nings lang,
To meet an' crack, an' sing a sang,
An' weet your pipes, for little wrang,
    To purse or person,
To sere* Johnnie Dowie's gang,
    There thrum a verse on.
O Dowie's Ale! thou art the thing
That gars us crack an' gat us sing,
Cast by our cares, our wants a' fling

Frae us wi' anger.
Thou e'en mak'st passion tak' the wing;
Or thou wilt bang'er.
How bless'd is he wha has a groat,
To spare upon the cheering pot;
He may look blyth as ony Scot
That e'er was born:
Gie's a' the like, but wi' a coat,
An' guide frae scorn.
But think na' that Strong Ale alone
Is a' that's kept by dainty John;
Na' na' for i' the place there's none
Frae end to end,
For meat can set you better on
Than can your friend.
Wi' looks as mild as mild can be,
An' smudgin' laugh, wi' winkin' ee,
An' lowly bow down to his knee
He'll say fu' douce,
'Whe gentlemen, stay till I see
'What's i' the house.'
—Anither bow—'Deed, gif ye please,
'Ye can get a bit toasted cheese,
'A crum o' tripe, ham, dish o' pease
(The season fitten)
'An egg, or cauler frae the seas
A fluck or whitten
'A nice beef-stake—or ye may get
'A gude buff'd herring, reisted skate
'An' means(?) an' (tho' past it's date)
'A cut o' veal
'Ha ha it's no' that unco late
'I'll do it weel.'
O G****y, R********, dreigh doun
An' antiquarian P**** soun',
Wi' mony ithers i' the town,
What wad come o'er ye
Gif Johnny Dowie shou'd stap down
To th' grave before ye?
Ye sure wad break your hearts wi' grief;

An' in Strong Ale find nae relief,
War ye to lose your Dowie— chief
    O' bottle keepers
Three years at least, now to be brief
    Ye'd gang wi' weepers(?)
But gude forbid! for your sakes a'
That sic an usefu' man should fa'
For frien's o' mine, between us twa,
    Right i' your lug.
You'd lose a houff baith warm an' braw
    An' unco snug.
Then pray for's health this mony a year,
Fresh three-'n-a-ha'penny, best o' beer
That can (tho' dull) you brawly cheer,
    Recant you weel up
An' gar you a' forget your wear
    Your sorrows seal up.
————————————'Another Bottle, John.'
'Gentlemen, 'tis past twelve, and time to go home.'
  (*sere = serious)

Merlin's Wynd. This ancient but vanished wynd owed its name to Walter Merlion, the French mason, who, in 1532, covered the High Street with its first paving and whose own chosen burial place in the mouth of the wynd was marked out by stones outlining a coffin lid. He was the master mason who in 1502 erected the vaulted gateway at Holyrood Abbey. The close disappeared when the Tron Kirk and Blair Street were built.

Old Provost's Close. In 1722 attention was drawn to the state of this close which was described as 'hung on both sides with a most nauseous piece of tapestry of puddens, tripes, livers, paunches and sheep-heads. Also nolt foot oil and paunch grease are boiled in the night time in several places in the close and fires have been caused—no cleansing is carried out'.

Stripping Close. 'Culprits who were whipped from the Castlehill to the Netherbow were stripped of their raiment at the head of this close . . . the chastisement ended at World's End Close'.

Tanner's Close. Here lived the infamous Burke & Hare, murderers. They lured their victims into the close and there brought their lives to an end, selling the bodies for dissection.

In his descriptions of 'Closes and Wynds of Old Edinburgh' detailed in a Volume of a *Book of the Old Edinburgh Club* Charles B. Boog Watson has delved thoroughly into aliases or derivations of close names. He has noted the following list of 30 names, however, as 'unidentified closes' to which he could offer no derivation possibly due to mistake, mis-spelling, or misnomer:

Adamesone's Clois
Ainslie's Close
Bell Close
Berwick's Close
Bois Wynd
Bonkill's Close
Bryden's Close
Dalgleish's Close
David Murray's Close
Dow's Close
Earl of Argyle's ('Eirle of Irgyllis) Close
Francis Bell's Close
Fullartoun's Close
George Smith's Close
George Wynd
Henry Nisbet's Close
John Hamilton's Close
Kincaid's Close
Lucky Thom's Close
Maitland's Lane
Master of Work's Close
Mein's Close
Morie's Close
Mr Thomas Rigg's Close
Patrick Edgar's Close

Pett Street' Close
Pitcairlie's Close
Scott's Close
Shennen Close
William Hiltray's Close

PART SIX

Appendix B

Appendix B consists of a list of most of the current close, court, etc., names quoting the previous obsolete name/names alongside.

Advocate's Close	Home's; Provost Stewart's; Sir James Stewart's
Allan's Close	Abernethy's; Dougal's; Douglas; Doul's; Dowel's; Duell's; Dunlop's; Leitche's; Leith's; Leithe's
Anchor Close	Anchor Tavern in Fuller's Close; Fordyce; Foular's; Fowlar's Fuller's
Bailie Fyfe's Close	Barrie's; Barry's; Cockburn's; Trotter's
Bakehouse Close	Cordiner's; Hammermen's; Huntly
Baron Maule's Close	Bassendyne's; Society
Bible Land	Shoemaker's
Bishop's Close	Alexander Lindsay's; Bishop's Land; Edward Nisbet's; James Nisbet's; Lindsay's; Patrick Nisbet's
Blair's Close	Baird's
Borthwick's Close	Lord Durie's
Boswell's Court	Lothian's
Brodie's Close	Baker's; Cullen's; Little's; Lord Cullen's; South End Entry to Old Bank Close
Brown's Close	Paterson's; Sommerville's
Bull's Close	Drummond's; Dr. Drummond's; Ford's Row; Lamont's Land; May Drummond's
Burnet's Close	Johnston's
Byres' Close	Lauder's; Malcolme's
Campbell's Close	Rae's
Cant's Close	Alexr. Cant's
Carrubber's Close	Carrutherber's
Chalmer's Close	Boyd's; Chamber's; Deasyre's; Densquer's; Densyre's
Craig's Close	Alexr. Dennistoun's; Birnie's;

	Carmichael's; Dennistoun's; Haliburton's; Josiah's; Joussie's; Joysie's
Dickson's Close	Aikman's; Dixon's
Fisher's Close	Hamilton's
Fleshmarket Close	Old Greenmarket; Provost's
Forsyth's Close	Gloucester Gate; Strachan's
Fountain Close	Bassendean's; Collington's; David Stevenson's; Fullarton's; John Barton's; Moubray's; Stevenson's
Geddes Entry	Hutcheson's; Richardson's
Gibb's Close	Robert Gibb's.
Gladstone Court	Bowling Green; Entry to Bowling Green; Magdalene Entry
Gullan's Close	Gillilan's; Gillons's; Goolan's; Goolen's
Hope's Court	Dr. Hope's
Hyndford's Close	Charteris; Collington's
James Court	Brownhill's Court; Fairden's; Fountainhall; Gladstane's; Jardine's; John Dickson of Hartree; Whitslade's
Lady Stair's Close	Lady Gray's; Stair's
Lochend Close	East Lochend's; Nether lochend's
Lyon's Close	Old Lyon's; Stalker's
Mary King's Close	Alexander King's; King's; Touris; Towris; Towrs
Mid Common Close	Common; Middle Common; Vietche's
Monteith's Close	Fleming's
Morrison's Close	Callender's; John Morison's
Mylne's Court	Cranston's
New Assembly Close	Back of Bell's Wynd; Commercial Bank; Fairlie's Entry from Cowgate; Murray's; Snawdoun's
North Foulis Close	Foulis; Fowler's; Fowlis
North Gray's Close	Gray's
Old Assembly Close	Assembly; Barnes'; Durie's; Gillespie's; Gillespy's; Little's;

	Patrick Shiell's; Steil's; Stiel's; Zair's
Old Fishmarket Close	Fishmarket; Fishmercate; Gourlay's; Humph's; Suittie's; Swift's
Old Playhouse Close	Dallas; Inglis; Upper Playhouse
Old Post Office Close	Barron's; Jacob Barron's; Little's; Old Post House
Old Stamp Office Close	Fortune's; Newbank; Old Bank; Old Ship; Ship; Ship Tavern
Paisley Close	East Bailie Fyfe's; Smith's
Panmure Close	McKell's
Reid's Close	Bailie Reid's; Haddington's Entry
Reid's Court	Blyth's; Reid's Coach Yard; Reid's Yard
Riddle's Court	John McMorran's; Macmorran's; Royston's; Shaw's; Sir John Smith's
Semple's Close	Sempill's; Williamson's
South Gray's Close	Coyne-house; Coynie; Mint
Stevenlaw's Close	Kennedy's; Stanelaw's; Stonelaw's; Tailyifiar's; Telfer's; Telpher's
Toddrick's Wynd	Toderick's
Trunk's Close	Bryson's; Purvis; Stirling's; Touring's
Tweeddale Court	Alexander Young's; James Brown's; John Laing's; Marquis of Tweeddale's; Tweedale's; Young's
Vallence's Entry	Vallen's; Vallene's; Valentine's
Wardrop's Court	Henderson's; Middle Baxter's
Warriston Close	Bruce's
White Horse Close	Davidson's; Laurence Ord's; Ord's
World's End Close	Stanfield's; Sweit's; Swift's

Appendix 'C' refers to William Edgar's first complete and accurate plan of Edinburgh in 1742 with a list of 35 Close, etc., names in existence at that date and still retaining the same names today; and 62 others long since obsolete but appearing on the plan.

Closes, etc., Still in existence today:

Advocate's Close
Allan's Close
Anchor Close
Bailie Fyfe's Close
Bell's Wynd
Borthwick's Close
Brown's Close
Bull's Close
Burnet's Close
Byres' Close
Cant's Close
Carrubber's Close
Chalmer's Close

Covenant Close
Dickson's Close
Fisher's Close
Fleshmarket Close
Fountain Close
Hyndford's Close
Jackson's Close
Lady Stair's Close
Lyon's Close
Mary King's Close
Monteith's Close
Morrison's Close
New Assembly

Close
Panmure Close
Riddle's Close
Skinner's Close
Toddrick's Wynd
Trunk's Close
Wardrop's Court
Warriston's Close
World's End
  Close
Writer's Court

Closes, etc., appearing on the plan but the names of which are no longer in existence today:

Assembly Close
Back of Best's
  Wynd
Back of
  Borthwick's
  Close
Barringer's Close
Best's Wynd
Blackfriar's Wynd
Carthrae's Close
Cap & Feather
  Close

Celler's Close
Con's Close
Craig's Close (1)
Craig's Close (2)
Curry's Close
Don's Close
Dr. Sinclair's
  Close
Dunbar's Close
Fishmarket Close
Forrester's Wynd
Fowlar's Close

Fowler's Close
Galloway's Close
Gosford's Close
Grant's Close
Gray's Close
Gray's (or Mint)
  Close
Halkerston's
  Wynd
Hart's Close
Hastie's Close
High School Close

Hutcheson's Close
Kennedy's Close
Kinloch's Close (1)
Kinloch's Close (2)
Libberton's Wynd
Lord Cullen's Close
Lord Streighan's Close
Lower Baxter's Court
Marlin's Wynd
Marquis of Tweeddale's Close
Middle Baxter's Court
Middle Fleshmarket Close
Mill's Square
Morocco Close
Murdoch's Close
Newbank Close
Niddry's Close
Old Bank Close
Old Post House Close
Paterson's Court
Pearson's Close
Peebles Wynd
Robertson's Close
Roxburgh's Close
Sandiland's Close
Scot's Close
Smith's Close
Stanelaw's Close
Steil's Close
Stewart's Close
Swan's Close
Upper Baxter's Close
Walter Willie's Close

Bibliography

AA Town and City Guides Edinburgh (1988)

Book of the Old Edinburgh Club various volumes (1923 on)

Charles B Boog Watson's *Closes and Wynds of Old Edinburgh*,
    contained in a Volume of a *Book of the Old Edinburgh Club*

Edinburgh, David Daiches (1977)

From Castle to Abbey, William Dick (1947)

Harper's Handbook to Edinburgh (1981)

History and Derivation of Edinburgh Street Names Edinburgh,
    Corporation, 1975

Lowlands of Scotland: Edinburgh and the South, Maurice Lindsay
    (1956)

Old and New Edinburgh, James Grant

The Buildings of Scotland: Edinburgh, Gifford, McWilliam, Walker,
    Wilson, 1984

The Scottish Borders and Edinburgh, Roger Smith (1983)

The Streets of Edinburgh by Edinburgh Impressions (1984)

The Writing on the Walls, Elizabeth Berry

Edinburgh 'Evening News'

Wm. Edgar's first complete and accurate plan of Edinburgh in
    1742

Edinburgh, Brian Bell (1989)

The Buildings of Edinburgh, A.F. Kersting & M. Lindsay (1981)

The Royal Mile, J. Crumley and M. Alexander (1989)

Epilogue

ANDREW GIBSON MACPHERSON,
Joiner and Cabinetmaker
Born 9/10/1864
Died /11/1935

Who, you may ask was Andrew Gibson Macpherson?

In the Prologue to this book I mentioned that my Grandfather was born in Chessel's Court and with other of my ancestors had lived in Carrubber's and White Horse Close.

Well . . . Andrew Gibson Macpherson was that man and I devote this brief memorial to him. Although I was very young when he died and sadly I never really got to know him I have been informed by other members of my family that he took a great interest in the area in which he was born and was only too pleased to impart his detailed knowledge of the 'nooks and crannies' in the Royal Mile to anyone ready to listen and walk the route of Kings, noblemen and ordinary folk with him.

I would like to feel that in some way, from 'a distance', he has helped me in my research and compilation of this book and I would like to think that it meets with his approval!

Index

Acheson House   83

Advocate's Close   23

Allan's Close   26

Anchor Close   27, 50

Bailie Fyfe's Close   32

Bakehouse Close   50

Baron Maule's Close   36

Bell's Wynd   63

Bible Land   38

Bishop's Close   31

Blair's Close   74

Borthwick's Close   66

Boswell's Court   73

Boyd, George   94

Brass Rubbing Centre
   (Chalmer's Close)   34

Brodie's Close   67

Brodie, William (Deacon)   67

Brown's Close   43

Bull's Close   49

Burns, Robert   108

Burnet's Close   64

Byres' Close   22

Camera Obscura
   i.e.(Outlook Tower)   77

Campbell's Close   43

Cannonball House   90

Canongate Church   82

Canongate Tolbooth   81

Cant's Close   60

Carrubber's Close   30

Chalmer's Close   34

Chessel's Court   55

City Chambers   77

Covenant Close   64

Craig's Close   27

Dickson's Close   60

Dunbar's Close   39

Fisher's Close   70

Fleshmarket Close   29

Forsyth's Close   46

Fountain Close   58

Galloway's Entry   46

Geddes Entry   28

Geddes, Sir Patrick   8

Gibb's Close   56

Gladstone Court   39

Gladstone's Land   77

Golfer's Land   43

Gullan's Close   57

High Kirk Of St Giles   87

Highland Church of Tolbooth
   (St John's)   90

Hope's Court   36

Hume, David   17

Huntly House   84

Hyndford's Close   58

Jackson's Close   29

James' Court   17

John Knox House   78

Jollie's Close   16

Lady Stair's Close   18

Little Lochend Close   42

Lochend Close   42

Lyon's Close   29

Mary King's Close   24

Melrose Close   60

Mercat Cross   87

Mid Common Close   37

Monteith's Close   36

Moray House   84

Morocco Land   37

Morrison's Close   31

Moubray House   78

Museum of Childhood   84

Mylne's Court   16

Netherbow Port   78

New Assembly Close   62

Nor' Loch 91
North Foulis Close 28
North Gray's Close 31
Old Assembly Close 64
Old Edinburgh Tolbooth 90
Old Fishmarket Close 66
Old Playhouse Close 54
Old Post Office Close 27
Old Stamp Office Close 29
Old Tolbooth Wynd 39
Outlook Tower 77
Paisley Close 32
Panmure Close 41
Parliament House 88
Parliament Square 89
Queensberry House 83
Reid's Close 49
Reid's Court 43
Riddle's Close & Court 71
St Giles' Cathedral 87

St John's Pend 53
St Margaret's Well 95/96
Semple's Close 16
Skinner's Close 16
South Gray's Close 59
Stevenlaw's Close 62
Sugarhouse Close 53
Toddrick's Wynd 60
Tron Kirk 85
Trunk's Close 36
Tweeddale Court 57
Vallence's Entry 49
Wardrop's Court 21
Warriston Close 23
White Horse Close 47
Whiteford House 46
World's End Close 57
Writer's Court 23
Writers Museum 18